There's
More
to
New Jersey
Than
the
Sopranos

LIBRARY OF CONGRESS CATALOGING-IN-PUBLICATION DATA

Mappen, Marc. There's more to New Jersey than the Sopranos / Marc Mappen.
    p.   cm.
Includes bibliographical references and index.
ISBN 978–0–8135–4586–8 (pbk. : alk. paper)
1. New Jersey—History.   I. Title.
F134.M126   2009
974.9—dc22

                                                                2008048066

A British Cataloging-in-Publication record for this book is available from the
British Library.

The quotation from August Kleinzahler in chapter one is from the book *Cutty One
Rock: Low Characters and Strange Places, Gently Explained* (New York: Farrar, Straus
& Giroux, 2004).

"New Jersey Hall of Fame Speech" by Bruce Springsteen. Copyright © 2008 Bruce
Springsteen. Reprinted by permission. International copyright secured. All rights
reserved.

Visit our Web site: http://rutgerspress.rutgers.edu

Manufactured in the United States of America

THIS BOOK IS DEDICATED to the wonderful New Jersey history community, which includes, among others, museum staff, historical-society members, volunteers, genealogists, reenactors, K–12 teachers, university faculty, archivists, archeologists, independent scholars, historic preservationists, and just plain history buffs, all of whom have come to regard our state's heritage as an important and fun field of study and seek to introduce their fellow citizens to that heritage.

CONTENTS

INTRODUCTION

An American tourist on vacation in Europe stopped at a restaurant in Gdansk, Poland, where she struck up a conversation with a local at the next table. "Where do you come from?" he asked. When she said she was from New Jersey, he replied with a smile of recognition, "Ah, Sopranos!"

Even for fans of that show (myself included), it is a bit disheartening that the first thing that pops into the mind of people around the world when they hear the name of our state is that television series about a dysfunctional crime family, set against a bleak and violent landscape.

New Jersey is actually an interesting little state, with quite a rich history of contributions to the modern world. Consider some of New Jersey's famous firsts. The phonograph, electric light, and movies were invented here, thanks to Thomas Edison. Also invented or improved in the Garden State were transistors, drive-in movies, Teflon, and decaffeinated coffee.

Two New Jersey engineers, John Roebling and his son Washington Roebling, designed and oversaw the construction of the Brooklyn Bridge, a marvel when it opened in 1883.

The first successful submarine, the first intercollegiate football game, the first baseball game played with modern rules all happened here. Atlantic City contributed saltwater taffy and the boardwalk to the world.

The first almost-complete dinosaur fossil was unearthed in New Jersey, and named the Hadrosaurus, in honor of the town of Haddonfield, where it was found.

The echo of the Big Bang—the cosmic event that marked the birth of our universe some 13.7 billion years ago—was first identified by scientists from Bell Labs in Murray Hill.

The state has been home to world-famous celebrities. My list of the top ten, in no particular order are:

Woodrow Wilson, twenty-eighth president of the United States

Albert Einstein, regarded as the world's most famous scientist

Thomas Edison, the world's most famous inventor

William Livingston, the first governor of the state of New Jersey and signer of the U.S. Constitution

Alice Paul, a Quaker girl from South Jersey who became a leading figure in the women's rights movement

Paul Robeson, athlete, scholar, entertainer, civil rights crusader

Frank Sinatra, a man who transformed American popular music

Count Basie, the brilliant jazz composer and performer

Selman Waksman, the scientist who invented one of the first modern wonder drugs, streptomycin

Molly Pitcher, the inspiring Revolutionary War heroine

New Jersey also has a rich cultural life, with twenty-nine professional theater companies, twenty-two professional orchestras, eight dance companies, and one of the biggest poetry festivals in the nation. There are more historic sites per square mile in New Jersey than in many other states noted for their history, like Pennsylvania, New York, and Virginia.

My purpose in this book is to explore some of the aspects of New Jersey that are largely unknown to those outside the state as well as to Jerseyans themselves. That's not to say that the book is meant as a celebratory bit of boosterism; on the contrary, I want to show the dark as well as the light, the good as well as the bad, the uplifting as well as the grotesque about our state.

The take-home message is simply this: there's more to New Jersey than the Sopranos!

———

Many of the chapters in this book originally appeared in the New Jersey section of the *New York Times*, in the magazine *New Jersey Heritage*, or as commentary on the radio program NewJerseytimes. My thanks to the staff of those venues for their assistance. Other chapters were originally speeches, for which my thanks to members of the audience whose reactions helped me revise the text. Chapter 40 is adapted from an invited lecture I gave as part of the Rutgers Ethics Initiative series, cosponsored by the Eagleton Institute of Politics and the Prudential Business Ethics Center at Rutgers. Professor Michael Rockland offered valuable advice. The staff of Rutgers University Press provided their customary high level of editorial oversight. The following institutions were extremely helpful in my quest for illustrations: the New Jersey State Archives, Rutgers University Special Collections, the Newark Public Library, and the library of the New Jersey Office of Legislative Services. Finally, I want to acknowledge the love and support of my wife, Ellen; son, Ben; and daughter, Rebecca.

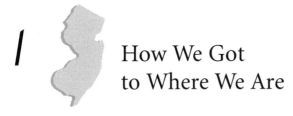

1 How We Got to Where We Are

What was it like, some twelve thousand years ago, when the ancestors of the Lenape Indians arrived in the land that, hundreds of generations later, was named New Jersey? Did these Stone Age people have watercraft that enabled them to travel over the river that we call the Delaware? Did they walk down the Hudson Valley? Did they come as a clan, with men, women, and children, or was it a party of male hunters following the track of game? One can imagine these people, the descendants of the Asians who crossed over to North America from Siberia, making their way cautiously but hopefully into our land of pine forests and lakes. However they arrived, they were the first human beings to settle here.

The arrival of Europeans can be dated to Giovanni da Verrazzano, an Italian in the employ of the king of France who explored the Atlantic coastline of North America in the ship *La Dauphine* in 1524, followed in 1609 by Henry Hudson, an Englishman hired by the Dutch, whose ship the *Half Moon* explored the Delaware and Hudson rivers. Following Hudson, the Dutch established their New Netherland colony, headquartered on Manhattan Island.

In 1664, fifty-five years after Henry Hudson, the New Netherland colony was conquered by the British. Back in England, the Duke of York, brother to the king, took a map of the former Dutch territory and selected a stretch of land between the Hudson River and the Delaware River, which he gave the name "New Jersey." The duke conveyed this land in a deed to two of his nobleman friends, Sir John Carteret and John Lord Berkeley, on June 24, 1664, which is as good a date as any to celebrate New Jersey's birthday. Carteret, incidentally, owned property on the isle of Jersey in the English Channel, where he had sheltered the king during the English Civil War. The name "New Jersey" was probably meant as a compliment to Sir John.

So a political entity named New Jersey began in the seventeenth century and has endured through the eighteenth, nineteenth, twentieth, and now into the twenty-first century. Certain themes have characterized New Jersey during much of that time.

The most obvious characteristic about New Jersey today, its population density, is not one of those enduring themes. We may have more people per square mile (1,138) than any other state and most other nations, including India and China. But this is a relatively new phenomenon dating from the post–World War II era when the federal highway system opened up the state for in-migration. Another relatively recent phenomenon is the state's wealth. The latest federal statistics show that New Jersey has the highest per capita income of any state, and if we were peeled off from the United States and made a separate country (not entirely a bad idea, in my view), we would be the wealthiest nation in the world. The rest of the United States would come in second, followed in third place by Luxembourg.

What has characterized New Jersey down the centuries are the following:

Diversity

Our state has an astonishing diversity. Geographers marvel at how many different types of landscape exist in our small area, including wetlands, mountains, coastal plains, and pine barrens. We have over twenty-six hundred species of flora—more than many larger states. A higher proportion of New Jersey is covered by forest (40 percent) than many other states, including California and Alaska. There are more horses per square mile here than in any other state in the nation; or if you were a horse you would say that there are fewer square miles per you than any other state.

The same diversity characterizes the human population of our state. In the colonial era, the population included Native Americans, Dutch, Finns, Swedes, Africans, English, and Scots. This diversity continued after the Revolution. In the early 1800s, came the Irish and the Germans; after the Civil War, came the Italians and the eastern Europeans. Today we are still a center for immigrants. The 2000 census shows that the foreign-

Immigrants

New Jersey has always had a diverse population, with a higher proportion of immigrants than the national average. This idealized 1887 image depicts immigrants coming to America through New York harbor; the coast of New Jersey can be glimpsed on the left. Library of Congress.

born in New Jersey constitute 18 percent of our population—the third highest in the nation, after California and New York, and about as high as it was during the Golden Age of Ellis Island a century ago. Every year since 1850, when the United States census first began to track the birthplace of residents, New Jersey has exceeded the national average in the percentage of foreign-born in the population.

But the number of foreign-born is only part of the picture. The census has a category called "immigrant stock," which adds together the number of foreign-born and their children born in this country. In 2000 the immigrant stock accounted for 28 percent of the population. One out of four New Jerseyans speaks a language other than English at home. It is this immigrant stock that is enabling New Jersey's population to grow rather than to shrink.

What has changed dramatically over the years is where New Jersey's immigrant population comes from. In 1880 the top five sending nations were all European: Ireland, Germany, Great Britain, Holland, and France. The top five sending nations today are all non-European: India, the Dominican Republic, Cuba, Mexico, and the Philippines. Seven out of ten of New Jersey's immigrants today come from Latin America or Asia. Hispanics are the fastest-growing group.

What this means for the future is that the percentage of non-Hispanic whites in the state's population will steadily decline, while all others (Hispanic whites, blacks, and Asians) will steadily increase. It has been estimated that in the year 2034, the European whites who have dominated New Jersey since the 1600s will no longer be a majority. It will be difficult to speak of anybody as a "minority" group member if there is no majority.

Will 2034 be traumatic in New Jersey? Probably not. It will simply be an extension of how immigrant groups have been absorbed into our society. A survey conducted in 2007 by Professor Cliff Zukin of Rutgers University measured the attitude of New Jerseyans toward population diversity. The survey showed a high level of tolerance in our state. Compared to the national average, New Jerseyans are far likelier to regard immigration as an asset than a burden. Zukin feels that the residents of our state have experienced population diversity firsthand and have developed a high degree of tolerance and a cheerful willingness to accept differences in others, a phenomenon he describes as a "whatever" attitude.

Transportation Crossroads

Throughout its history New Jersey has been a crossroads state—the land that had to be traversed by any person or product traveling from New York to Philadelphia, or from New England to the South. During the Revolutionary War, when Philadelphia was the capital of the rebellious colonies and New York was the de facto British capital, more battles were fought in New Jersey than in any other state. During the canal-building craze of the early 1800s, New Jersey built the Morris Canal and the Delaware and Raritan Canal. In 1825 the engineer and inventor John Stevens built a working steam railroad—the first in the nation—on his

Transportation Corridor
The Camden & Amboy Railroad was a key link in the early American transportation network, carrying passengers between New York and Philadelphia. Special Collections and University Archives, Rutgers University Libraries.

property in Hoboken. Stevens was also one of the pioneers of the steamboat industry, and his vessels plied the Delaware and the Hudson. Incidentally, one of the few accounts of early train travel in New Jersey comes from one of the great writers of all time, Charles Dickens. The English novelist made a trip to America in 1842, and like everybody else traveling from New York City to Philadelphia by rail in the nineteenth century, he took the train through New Jersey. His recollection of that ride is contained in his book *American Notes*. What struck Dickens most forcefully was the enthusiasm with which his fellow riders spit out the window, which he described tartly as "a playful and incessant shower of expectoration."

One indication of the movement of people in and out of New Jersey is the number of famous people who came here from the outside—like Woodrow Wilson from Virginia, Thomas Edison from Ohio, and Albert Einstein from Germany—as well as those born here who moved away to earn fame elsewhere—like Grover Cleveland, James Fenimore Cooper, and Frank Sinatra. The geographical centrality of New Jersey is why so many immigrants have settled here, whether they came first to Ellis Island in the twentieth century or to Newark Liberty Airport in the twenty-first.

In its 8,722 square miles, New Jersey has spawned 566 municipalities cheek by jowl to each other. Most are small; dozens are less than five square miles in area. The smallest, weighing in at one-tenth of a square mile, is Loch Arbour Village in Monmouth County. In all, our state has .076 municipalities per square mile—the highest density of any state. These communities stoutly defend their autonomy.

This devotion to home rule stretches back into the New Jersey past. The 1664 deed from the Duke of York to his supporters placed authority over the land and government to shareholders, known as the proprietors. But the situation was clouded by the fact that many of the settlers who came here challenged the proprietors' authority. As these settlers saw it, they had the right to the land through Indian deeds, squatters' rights, and conflicting grants from the government of New York. The proprietors, who controlled the government of New Jersey, resisted these counter-claims. This was a stressful situation in which the residents of towns and villages could not go to sleep at night with the assurance that they had a lawful right to the land they lived on. The result was a history of violent protest in the seventeenth and eighteenth centuries waged by towns-people against the colonial government and the proprietors. This was re-inforced by the strong community focus of Presbyterians and Quakers—religions prominent in New Jersey's early years.

Given this legacy, it is no surprise that in the centuries that followed, New Jersey laws gave towns protection from the intrusion of state govern-ment. In the nineteenth century, legislation was adopted giving munici-palities authority over their schools. The 1917 Home Rule Act gave many additional powers to municipalities, and the current state constitution, adopted in 1947, declares that "The provisions of this Constitution and of any law concerning municipal corporations formed for local govern-ment, or concerning counties, shall be liberally construed in their favor."

Critics charge that this fierce localism is unnecessarily costly, since most municipalities have their own mayor, school board, fire depart-ment, police, and emergency services, and that this duplication of local services contributes to the state's crushing property-tax burden, the highest in the nation. An example of this waste is the claim that there is more fire equipment in Bergen County than in all of New York City. It is also claimed that home rule contributes to corruption, on the theory that bribery is easier at a local level. One critic of home rule, the noted political leader Alan Karcher, described this situation as New Jersey's "multiple municipal madness." Defenders of home rule argue that it provides democracy at the local level, giving residents a powerful voice in how their communities are governed.

But whether for good or ill, this situation is likely to endure into the future. Politicians in this state quickly learn that tampering with home rule is political suicide, and reform efforts have always failed. Karcher is a case in point—he did not criticize the system until he had left office as Speaker of the Assembly.

The North–South Split

Besides 566 municipalities and twenty-one counties, New Jersey has two distinct regions—North and South—whose differences date far into the past. During the Ice Age, glaciers covered the northern half of the state, leaving the two regions distinct in their topography and vegetation. Traveling south on the Garden State Parkway, you can see this legacy as the ground on the side of the road abruptly becomes sandier and the pine trees smaller.

Back before the arrival of Europeans, there were two different groups of Lenape in the land that was to become New Jersey—the Munsee in the North and the Unami in the South. They spoke different dialects of the Delaware language, and ethnographers are unsure whether they could even understand each other. It eerily foreshadows the sometimes strained communication between the North and South that has continued to characterize the state.

Soon after the colony of New Jersey was established by the English, it was divided into two separate colonies—East and West Jersey, each with its own governor, legislature, and proprietary body with authority over the land. The East Jersey capital was Perth Amboy and the West Jersey

Map of New Jersey in 1777
Although this map was published seventy-five years after East Jersey and
West Jersey were combined into a single colony, it still refers to "the
Jerseys" and displays the old dividing lines that run diagonally from the
northwest to the southeast. This regionalism has continued to the present
day. New Jersey State Archives, Department of State.

capital was Burlington. The border between East and West Jersey was a diagonal line drawn from the Delaware Water Gap in the northwest to Little Egg Harbor in the southeast, so that the land area we today call South Jersey corresponds pretty closely to the old colony of West Jersey, and today's North Jersey translates into the colony of East Jersey.

The two colonies were brought together by the British Crown in 1703, but there was still a strong separatism. Even though there was now one governor and one legislature, the government continued to move back and forth between the two capitals. For generations, Americans (George Washington among them), referred to our state in the plural as "the Jerseys." The East Jersey board of proprietors lasted until 1998; the West Jersey board is still in existence and is the oldest corporation in the United States.

There is today a certain degree of animosity from South Jersey toward the North—the feeling that the South does not get its share—and not so long ago there was a succession movement in South Jersey. It was not entirely in jest.

The North–South division of the state has been exacerbated by the existence of two of the nation's largest cities at either end—New York in the north and Philadelphia in the south. It may have been Benjamin Franklin, that wise founding father, who first humorously described New Jersey as a "barrel tapped at both ends." Whoever said it was right on the money. These two urban areas exert a strong cultural influence over our state. As the historian John Cunningham put it: "The rising sun throws New York's shadow over the state, the setting sun bathes New Jersey in the shadow of Philadelphia."

During the colonial era the British Crown forbade the establishment of a printing press in New Jersey, which made us dependent on newspapers from New York and Philadelphia. In the early twentieth century, Governor Woodrow Wilson lamented how commuters who resided in New Jersey got their news from out of state. The situation has not changed. In New Jersey there is still no statewide newspaper, no NBC, CBS, or ABC television station of our own. (Delaware is the only other state with no network affiliate.) Jerseyans who reside in the north watch

New York television stations, listen to New York radio stations, and root for New York teams. For South Jersey, simply substitute Philadelphia for New York.

The New Jersey Character

Every Jerseyan knows of the negative view of our state, and of the endless stream of Jersey jokes, like the classic line in Woody Allen's 1973 movie *Sleeper* where he gives his philosophic view of existence: "I believe that there's an intelligence to the universe, with the exception of certain parts of New Jersey." The deep roots of these putdowns can be seen in an off-hand comment in an 1872 issue of *Picturesque America* magazine that from its beginning New Jersey "has been the butt of sarcasm and wit of those who live outside her borders." Another is the recollection of a journalist writing in 1905 that back in the middle of the previous century, New Yorkers would speak of "the United States and New Jersey." Like the tip of an iceberg, these two remarks hint at a vast, subsurface tradition of dissing New Jersey that dates far back into the past.

This tradition has continued into the present. In 2002 a British professor of psychology, Richard Weisman, conducted an experiment to discover what makes people around the world laugh. He and his colleagues at the University of Hertfordshire sent out forty thousand jokes on the Internet, and asked readers to rank them on a scale of one to five. He received some two million votes from seventy different countries around the world, and the following joke emerged as the one with the highest score, and hence is officially the funniest in the world.

> A couple of New Jersey hunters are out in the woods when one of them falls to the ground. He doesn't seem to be breathing; his eyes are rolled back in his head.
>
> The other guy whips out his cell phone and calls the emergency services. He gasps to the operator: "My friend is dead! What can I do?"
>
> The operator, in a calm, soothing voice, says: "Just take it easy. I can help. First, let's make sure he's dead."
>
> There is a silence, then a shot is heard. The guy's voice comes back on the line. He says: "Okay, now what?"

What helps to make this story funny is that at the outset it announces that the setting is New Jersey, which telegraphs to the reader that something hilariously dumb is about to happen.

Why this enduring condescending attitude toward our little state? Several of the American colonies, like Massachusetts and Pennsylvania, were founded by religious groups as holy commonwealths, societies on a mission from God. Others produced a wealthy upper class with a taste for culture and refinement, like the planter aristocrats of Virginia or the merchants and patroons of New York. The western boundaries of most colonies were undefined, so that up until the formation of a national government, New York, Pennsylvania, Virginia, and other colonies could legitimately claim to be empires that stretched westward to the Mississippi River.

But from the start New Jersey was different from those other colonies. When the colony was founded in 1664, it was essentially a real estate speculation, with no divine mission or elite class. The colony consisted of farms and small villages; we did not have a major city such as Boston, New York, Philadelphia, or Charleston with their powerful religious, economic, and cultural elites that could boast of their importance in the solar system. Any dreams of territorial expansion westward were blocked by the fact that the colony was bounded on the west by the unmovable barricade of Pennsylvania.

And again, split between the New York and Philadelphia regions our identity has been shaped by outsiders. Ever since Babylon, urban elites have looked down their noses at the rural hinterland, and regarded the inhabitants of those hinterlands, at best, as their social inferiors or, at worst, as hopeless rubes.

What does this portrait of New Jersey, mostly painted by outsiders, look like? One of the royal governors sent here by the British Crown was Jonathan Belcher, who served from 1748 to 1757. He had been born to a wealthy New England family and had lived for a time in the luxury of the royal court in England. His first assignment as governor was Massachusetts. When he came to New Jersey, he was clearly appalled by the contrast with the high-society life he had lived in Boston and London. He found

New Jersey to be a stifling place of little culture or refinement. But on the positive side, clearly trying to say something nice, he remarked that it was "the best country I have seen for middling fortunes, and for people who have to live by the sweat of their brow." In other words, he was describing New Jersey as an unpretentious, blue-collar kind of place.

Much has changed since Belcher. New Jersey became a state within the new American nation, new waves of immigrants settled here, the industrial revolution transformed the landscape, and we changed from a rural to an urban society. And yet, that image of New Jersey has endured. It can be seen in the gritty, working-class lyrics of Bruce Springsteen and, yes, in the grim dog-whack-dog world of Tony Soprano. Consider how the *New York Times* described State Senator Richard J. Codey: "A bona fide Jersey guy, complete with rumpled suits, comb-over and a spaghetti-and-meatballs belly." Surely New York has politicians who are equally unfashionable in their appearance, but the newspaper blithely regarded these characteristics as quintessential Jerseyness.

We have internalized this view, and have come to regard ourselves in that light. This is not to say that New Jerseyans dislike their state. In fact, opinion polls find that a thumping two-thirds of residents rate the state as a good or excellent place to live. What we have done, though, is to take a perverse sort of pride in our ordinariness. In their book *Looking for America on the New Jersey Turnpike*, Rutgers professors Angus Gillespie and Michael Rockland conclude that residents of the state glory in the plain ugliness of that celebrated highway with a "So Bad, It's Good" attitude, an attitude that extends to other aspects of life in the Garden State. On display in the New Jersey Museum of Agriculture is a curious artifact that attests to the long history of that gentle self-mockery. It is a door from a Vernon, New Jersey, tavern, perhaps dating from the 1820s. On one side of the door is the painted image of a goofy, grinning country bumpkin wreathed in smoke from his cigar. Over his head are the words "I Live in Jersey." (On the reverse side is an unflattering caricature of a New Yorker.)

It is risky to try to define the character of a nation or a people, and even riskier to do it for a subdivision such as a state. But a New Jersey-

I Live in New Jersey

This self-mocking illustration of a New Jersey man was painted on the door of a tavern in Vernon, New Jersey, in the early nineteenth century. The door is on display at the New Jersey Museum of Agriculture. Photograph by the author.

born poet, August Kleinzahler, took a stab at it in a recent memoir of growing up in North Jersey: "The New Jersey character—at least this part of Jersey—is straightforward, plainspoken to the point of bluntness, though not at all unfriendly. The humor is deadpan, ironical, playfully deprecating. It's a beer-and-a-bump kind of place. Affectation is quickly and viscerally registered. There's a swagger, a bluff air of menace that many of the males wear. Sinatra is a caricature of it."

Kleinzahler is certainly right about the Sinatra part. The song that personifies Old Blue Eyes' life, "I Did It My Way," could be the New Jersey state song. (This suggestion is not made lightly—New Jersey is the only state that does not have an official state song, and the Sinatra tune could fill the bill.)

These aspects of the New Jersey character are widely recognized outside our state; *Time* magazine observed, "Other then Texas, Jersey is the only state to have a cohesive, distinct personality."

It is surely Bruce Springsteen, born and raised in Freehold, who best exemplifies the New Jersey state of mind. When he was inducted into the New Jersey Hall of Fame in 2008, he offered the audience a speech he described as a "Garden State Benediction," which strikingly reflects the longstanding low-brow image of our state, and the sarcastic but affectionate kind of pride that New Jerseyans take in that image:

> Rise up my fellow New Jerseyans, for we are all members of a confused but noble race. We, of the state that will never get any respect. We, who bear the coolness of the forever uncool. The chip on our shoulders of those with forever something to prove. And even with this wonderful Hall of Fame, we know that there's another bad Jersey joke coming just around the corner.
>
> But fear not. This is not our curse. It is our blessing. For this is what imbues us with our fighting spirit. That we may salute the world forever with the Jersey state bird, and that the fumes from our great northern industrial area to the ocean breezes of Cape May fill us with the raw hunger, the naked ambition and the desire not just to do our best, but to stick it in your face.

Amen to that, brother.

2

When Prehistoric Elephants Roamed New Jersey

On a winter day in 1954, a workman dredging a pond in Sussex County came upon the enormous, grinning skull of some monstrous animal. The owner of the pond, Gus Ohberg, called the police, who called the New Jersey State Museum in Trenton. After weeks of digging, scientists and volunteers unearthed the skeleton of a mastodon from the muck at the bottom of the pond. That skeleton now stands in the State Museum.

There have been more than a dozen other mastodon skeletons dug up in New Jersey over the years, plus countless teeth, tusks, and bone fragments. Jersey mastodons are on display in the Rutgers Geology Museum, the Harvard Museum of Comparative Zoology, the Bergen County Museum, and the Sussex County Historical Society.

Jersey fossil hunters have also uncovered some tooth fragments from mammoths, another species of prehistoric elephant. Mastodons and mammoths, incidentally, often get mixed up in the public mind. (It doesn't help that, for some perverse reason, the scientific name for mastodon is "mammut.") Basically, mammoths were bigger and hairier than mastodons, but the distinction would probably be of little concern if you bumped into one in prehistoric New Jersey.

Mastodons and mammoths came to North America about twenty-five million years ago across the land bridge between Alaska and Siberia. They seem to have been particularly fond of the chilly, Ice Age forests of eastern North America, including New Jersey, where they grazed on twigs, branches, pine cones, and grass.

Scientists estimate that mastodons and mammoths became extinct somewhere between five thousand and ten thousand years ago. This is practically yesterday as these things are measured. It used to be thought (by Thomas Jefferson, among other people) that these creatures might still be found alive somewhere in remote areas of Asia or North America.

Mastodon Skeleton
The fossilized remains of a New Jersey mastodon are exhibited in the Rutgers Geology Museum. Special Collections and University Archives, Rutgers University Libraries.

This romantic idea turned out to be false, but several carcasses of mammoths have been found frozen in Siberian ice, so fresh that once defrosted their flesh has been eagerly devoured by sled dogs.

Why did mastodons and mammoths die out? There have been many theories. Perhaps it was a change in climate, or the development of a genetic defect, or the spread of a fatal epidemic. It might also have been the work of some fierce and unrelenting predator who hunted down and killed every last one without concern for the environment or conservation. Guess who.

Yes, the age of the mastodon and the mammoth overlapped ours, and the creatures were here when humans first arrived in North America from Asia. Hungry, carnivorous humans, armed with spears, clubs, and nerve, were surely able to overcome those lumbering vegetarians. Using fire, hunters may have driven the beasts over cliffs; or perhaps they singled out infants for slaughter.

The idea that humans lived at the same time as mastodons and mammoths is intriguing. It helps to make up for the disappointing fact that, contrary to the old Hollywood B-movie images of sexy babes in fur bikinis battling tyrannosaurs, the last dinosaur became extinct millions of years before the first *Homo sapiens.*

The connection between humans and prehistoric elephants thousands of years ago brings us to the subject of two controversial artifacts found just across the New Jersey border in Delaware and Pennsylvania.

In the late nineteenth century a collector purchased a hoard of Indian relics said to have been unearthed from a farm in Bucks County, Pennsylvania. One of the objects was a broken piece of flat stone; it had evidently been used as a neck ornament. What made it remarkable was that engraved on one side was what appeared to be a mammoth smashing through an Indian village.

The artifact was defended as genuine by a wealthy amateur naturalist, Henry Chapman Mercer. In 1885 Mercer published "The Lenape Stone; or the Indian and the Mammoth" to argue his case. But it is the consensus of opinion among experts that the Lenape Stone is a fake. The ornament is of a type that dates from about 1,000 b.c., long after the mammoths died out. The stone is in two pieces, and lines that start on one piece do not match those on the other, indicating that the picture was drawn after the object was broken. The picture is also inaccurate: the feathers, tepees, and bows and arrows of the Indians depicted on the stone are closer to Buffalo Bill's Wild West show than to the Ice Age culture of the Delaware Valley. To the modern eye it looks like Godzilla trampling Tokyo. A Harvard archeologist, Stephen Williams, observed that it is hard to look at the Lenape Stone without guffawing.

The Holly Oak pendant is less easy to dismiss. In 1890 yet another well-to-do amateur naturalist, Hilborne T. Cresson, announced that he had discovered a prehistoric pendant made of sea shell near the Delaware town of Holly Oak. Engraved on the object was the clear, unmistakable image of a mammoth.

When it was first announced by Cresson, the Holly Oak pendant, like the Lenape Stone, was dismissed as a fake. It was then pretty much forgotten until the 1970s, when a geologist and an archeologist retrieved it from a neglected drawer in the Smithsonian and claimed in a cover story in the prestigious journal *Science* that, based on modern scientific evidence, the artifact was a real rendering of a mammoth, made by a prehistoric artist.

The debate continued to burn in scholarly journals. The anti-Holly Oak crowd has attacked the pendant on several grounds. They point to the character of Hilborne T. Cresson himself. Not long after announcing his discovery, he was fired from an archeological dig in Ohio for stealing specimens. Three years later, apparently quite mad, he blew his brains out with a pistol in a New York City park. He left behind a suicide note in which he babbled in a confused fashion about counterfeiting money.

The image on the pendant is suspiciously close to a genuine prehistoric bone engraving of a mammoth found in a cave in France in 1864. The anti-Holly Oak scientists charge that Cresson had a picture of the well-known French original in front of him when he counterfeited his pendant.

What appears to be the final word in the debate came in 1988, when the skeptics subjected the Holly Oak pendant to radiocarbon analysis. It was found to date from around A.D. 885, off by one hundred centuries from the age of the mammoths and mastodons.

So the Holly Oak pendant and the Lenape Stone are evidently frauds. But the fossils that have cropped up in New Jersey for the last few hundred years are genuine, and prove that those great beasts once roamed our state. There are no doubt more fossils to be found; maybe a dead mastodon is lurking under the zinnia bed next to your patio.

3 New Jersey Was Paradise

When outsiders make jokes about New Jersey, we get defensive. We talk about our beautiful woodlands and scenic shore.

Delaware Water Gap from New Jersey
This photograph, taken circa 1900, provides a hint of what New Jersey must have looked like to the first European explorers and settlers.
Library of Congress.

But let's face it—we're doing a pretty good job of fouling segments of our landscape with cheap strip malls, garish condo developments, decaying cities, traffic-clogged highways, bad air, and polluted water.

It was not always this way. Let's look at New Jersey the way the first Europeans saw it. To them, New Jersey was a paradise of beauty and abundance, even allowing for exaggeration.

Robert Juet was an officer on Henry Hudson's ship, the *Half Moon*, when it sailed from Holland to the New World in 1609. As the ship explored the coastline of what was to become New Jersey, Juet wrote in his journal: "This is a very good Land to fall with, and a pleasant Land to see."

Hudson sent five of his crewmen in a rowboat to explore the shore. Juet wrote down their report: "The Lands they told us were as pleasant with Grasse and Flowers, and goodly Trees, as ever they had seene, and very sweet smells came from them."

The Dutch who followed Henry Hudson established the colony of New Netherland, which included the present New Jersey and New York. One of those early Dutchmen who owned land on Staten Island and in New Jersey, David De Vries, described the abundance of wildlife. "There are elks, chiefly in the mountains; also hares, but they are not larger than the rabbits in Holland; foxes in abundance, multitudes of wolves, wild cats, squirrels—black as pitch, and gray, also flying squirrels—beavers in great numbers, minks, otters, polecats, bears, and many kinds of fur-bearing animals, which I cannot name or think of." De Vries wrote of the extremes of temperature, and how from the mountains a "pure, clear air" blew over the land.

Around Newark Bay he saw numberless wading birds, geese, cranes, partridges, and swans. He described wild turkeys weighing up to forty pounds. "Turtle-doves, at the time of year when they migrate, are so numerous, that the light can hardly be discerned where they fly." Black birds were so thick that he saw a man on Manhattan Island kill eighty-four with one shot from a musket.

De Vries saw the ocean teeming with fish. "There are many kinds of fish which we have not in our fatherland, so that I cannot name them all. In fresh waters, are pike, perch, and trout. There are fine oysters, large and small, in great abundance. In the summer-time crabs come on the flat shores, of very good taste. Their claws are the color of the flag of our Prince, orange, white and blue, so that the crabs show sufficiently that we ought to people the country, and that it belongs to us."

Another part of the environment was the Indians. Some of the Europeans thought the natives worshipped the Devil, and because Indian marriage customs were different from those of seventeenth-century Europe, they thought that Indian women were prostitutes. The Dutch named a river in nearby Delaware "Horrenkill" (Prostitute's River).

But the first European settlers also found much to admire in the way the Indians seemed to live in harmony with nature. One early Dutchman wrote, "It is somewhat strange that among these most barbarous people, there are few or none cross-eyed, blind, crippled, lame, hunch-backed or limping men; all are well-fashioned people, strong and sound of body, well-fed, without blemish."

With the English conquest of New Netherland in 1664, British settlers came to New Jersey in great numbers to build farms. They found the land well-suited for agriculture: level and watered by abundant rivers. Ester Huckens, a Quaker woman who settled in West Jersey, wrote a letter in 1676 to attract her friends to the New World: "Here is great store of Fish and Fowl, and plenty of Corn, and Cows, Hoggs, Horses, Oxen, Sheep, Venison, Nuts, Strawberries, Grapes, and Peaches; here is good English Wheat ripe in three Months."

Another Quaker, Richard Hartshorne, wrote: "We make our Soap & Candles, & all such things our selves; and in the winter we make good fires, and eat good meat; and our Women & Children are healthy; Sugar is cheap, Venison, Geese, Turkies, Pidgeons, Fowle & Fish plenty. . . . In short, this is a rare place for any poor man or others; and I am satisfied people may live better here then they do in Old England."

It is hard to imagine how unpopulated the land was, even after the arrival of the English. A traveler who walked through western New Jersey in 1672 wrote: "We have travelled a whole day together without seeing man or woman, house or dwelling-place."

In 1748 Peter Kalm, a Swedish scientist, toured the English colonies. On a coach ride through New Jersey he met an old man who could recall that fifty years before, there were no more than three farms between Trenton and New Brunswick.

Kalm observed that the route was now filled with farms, and he remarked that the countryside seemed more heavily populated than any part of the American colonies. But he still found it a land of abundance. He described the scene from the coach: "Near almost every farm was a spacious orchard full of peaches and apple-trees, and in some of them the fruit was fallen from the trees in such quantities as to cover nearly the whole surface. Part of it they left to rot, since they could not take it all in and consume it. Wherever we passed by, we were always welcome to go into the fine orchards, and gather our pockets full of the choicest fruit, without the possessor's so much as looking after it."

At the time Peter Kalm made his coach trip, New Jersey had a population of about sixty-one thousand. By Kalm's standards, that was large; by ours, it was astonishingly small. Today sixty-one thousand people is about the average attendance at a football game in the Meadowlands.

New Jersey remained largely rural for many generations. The poet John Masefield recalled how, as a young man at the close of the nineteenth century, he would row a boat across the Hudson from Manhattan and climb the Palisades where he could see "undisturbed primeval woods, with lonely farms stretching out beyond into a limitless west." The writer Earl Schenk Miers recalled that when he grew up in Middlesex County in the twentieth century, farms stretched for miles around his family home.

It was not until the post–World War II era that the cities spilled people out into the countryside, making both the city and the countryside worse. If you grew up in New Jersey you probably remember some stretch of rural countryside you knew as a child that is now paved over.

Today the land that Hartshorne, Jouet, De Vries, Kalm, and the others knew is pretty much gone; their accounts are now only dead words on old paper.

Weep for the New Jersey that we have lost; preserve what remains.

4 Move Over, Betsy Ross

Consider the flag of the United States, with its combination of stars and stripes. No matter what our political persuasion, region of the country, or ethnic group, we are united by Old Glory. It conjures up images of marines in World War II raising the flag on Iwo Jima, of Lincoln at Gettysburg, of immigrants coming to Ellis Island to become American citizens, of American astronauts on the moon.

Francis Hopkinson
This multitalented New Jersey signer of the Declaration of Independence is credited with designing the American flag. Special Collections and University Archives, Rutgers University Libraries – New Jersey Portraits Collection.

Our flag was born when our nation was born—during the American Revolution. We all know, or should know, the important role New Jersey played in the war of independence. Our little state was the crossroads of the Revolution, where George Washington and the Continental Army spent the major portion of the war and where more battles were fought than any other state. Indeed, the Battle of Trenton has been called the most important American victory ever, for the simple reason that if we had lost, it is likely there would be no America.

On the bicentennial of the Declaration of Independence in 1976, Governor Brendan Byrne was in Philadelphia for a commemorative event. In his speech he cracked that during the Revolution, New Jersey did the fighting, while Pennsylvania handled the paperwork.

But as a matter of fact, not all our state's contributions to the struggle were obtained on the battlefield. A New Jersey patriot, Francis Hopkinson of Bordentown (1737–1791), played a role—what the heck, played the essential role in creating our national flag.

Who was Francis Hopkinson? He does not fit the image of a hero. John Adams described him in 1776 as a "curious gentleman." "He is one of your pretty little, curious, ingenious Men. His Head is not bigger, than a large Apple. . . . I have not met with any Thing in natural History much more amusing and entertaining, than his personal Appearance. Yet he is genteel and well bred, and is very social."

Hopkinson was a prolific author, as well as a poet and painter. He also composed music and played several instruments, including the organ and the harpsichord. He wrote the song that is regarded as the first secular art song in America, "My Days Have Been So Wondrous Free." You get the feeling that if he were alive today, he would have his own Web site, blog, and garage band.

Hopkinson had a sharp sense of humor, perhaps best exemplified in his 1778 mock epic poem, "The Battle of the Kegs." It chronicles how, at one point in the Revolution, British soldiers fired in a panic at barrels floating down the Delaware River, thinking they were somehow dangerous. One stanza went:

> The cannons roar from shore to shore,
> The small arms make a rattle;
> Since wars began I'm sure no man
> E're saw so strange a battle.

Another stanza makes fun of the British commander, William Howe, who at the time of the kegs incident was in the midst of an affair with the wife of one of his officers.

Sir William he, snug as a flea,
Lay all this time a-snoring,
Nor dreamed of harm, as he lay warm,
In bed with Mrs. Loring.
Now in a fright he starts upright,
Awaked by such a clatter;
He rubs his eyes and boldly cries,
For God's sake what's the matter?

But despite Hopkinson's dabbling in the arts, you should not for a minute consider him a gadfly. A member of the first graduating class of the University of Pennsylvania, he was a lawyer and businessman. He served in the governor's council when New Jersey was a colony. But when the war came along he joined the rebel cause. He represented New Jersey in the Continental Congress, and was a signer of the Declaration of Independence. He also served in the wartime government, later becoming a respected judge.

In short, he was a man of so many talents you could consider him a New Jersey version of Leonardo da Vinci.

So now, what about the flag business? Well, on June 14, 1777, the Continental Congress adopted a resolution:

Resolved, that the flag of the thirteen United States be thirteen stripes, alternate red and white; that the union be thirteen stars, white in a blue field, representing a new constellation.

It was a historic vote, and June 14 has been celebrated ever afterward as Flag Day. But the resolution does not say who actually designed that flag.

You may be thinking to yourself, "Hey, wasn't it Betsy Ross?" And indeed, for a long time it was a staple of American patriotic lore that the young Philadelphia seamstress, in consultation with George Washington, designed and sewed that first flag. But in fact the Betsy Ross flag story came out nearly a century later from a grandson who was eleven years old when Betsy died. It is fair to say that most historians who have studied the issue dismiss the Betsy Ross legend. But you are certainly welcome to visit the Betsy Ross House or click on their Web site to decide for yourself.

The only person alive at the time who claimed credit for designing the flag was Hopkinson. In 1780, three years after the flag resolution, he presented the Continental Admiralty Board with a request to be compensated for the design work he had done for the new nation, which included a Great Seal of the United States, aspects of Continental currency, a seal for the board of the admiralty and . . . the flag of the United States of America. Hopkinson wrote, "For these services I have as yet made no Charge, nor received any Recompense. I now submit to your Honors' consideration, whether a quarter cask of the public wine will not be a proper and reasonable reward for these labours of fancy and a suitable encouragement to future exertions of a like nature."

(Why wine? Presumably because Continental currency was so debased at that point that Hopkinson may have preferred getting a commodity rather than a nearly worthless piece of paper.)

Hopkinson's request for compensation was approved by the Admiralty board and sent on to Congress for payment, but it was ultimately turned down by the Treasury board. It is important to note that it was not turned down because Hopkinson's claim to designing the flag was questioned, but rather because it was felt that this design work was the kind of thing that gentlemen receiving salary from the government should do as a matter of course, and that Hopkinson had not asked for compensation when he took on these assignments. It seems there was some friction between Hopkinson and the Treasury board over previous financial matters. So he didn't get his quarter cask of wine, but again, nobody questioned his work on the flag.

The question is: what *was* his design? Alas, no sketch from the Continental Congress's vote survives. But it is possible to figure it out.

Early on in the Revolution, some on the patriot side used a flag consisting of thirteen horizontal stripes, representing the colonies. In the union—the upper inner corner—these early rebel flags featured the two crosses that serve as the symbol of Great Britain. This was all very well when we imagined we were still loyal subjects of the king, only fighting against the tyranny of Parliament. But once we took the final step and declared our independence from England, something else had to go in that union. Hopkinson's inspiration was to put in stars.

As corroborating evidence that it was Hopkinson's inspiration to add the stars to the stars and stripes, his supporters cite the fact that his family seal contains stars as part of the design, and that Hopkinson used stars on several other of his design projects, including his sketch of a Great Seal for the Continental Board of War and Ordinance.

Flag experts (who are called by the fancy name "vexillologists") think that Hopkinson's original design had a staggered pattern of stars, a row of three, then two, then three, then two—for a total of thirteen. Vexillologists call this a "quincuncial" pattern. Some people later tinkered with the design, with a common variant having the stars in a circle.

Hopkinson died in 1791 at the young age of fifty-three. Too bad he didn't live a longer life. We can imagine that in a time of peace he might have written more about his work on the flag, and thus might have shed some of his obscurity to take his place among the Founding Fathers who lived longer, like Jefferson, Madison, and Adams. Like them, he was a patriot who, to quote the Declaration of Independence, risked his life, his fortune, and his sacred honor to create our nation. When you look at our national flag today, pause and think of Francis Hopkinson of Bordentown, New Jersey.

5   Good Golly, Miss Molly

coauthored with David Martin

Molly Pitcher is a name well-known in New Jersey and around the nation as the Revolutionary War heroine who, at the Battle of Monmouth in 1778, brought water to the thirsty American troops and took up arms against the British enemy. An Internet search on Google turns up 15,600 results for "Molly Pitcher," higher than for other notable figures of the Revolution like Baron Von Steuben, Nathanael Greene, Lord Cornwallis, and John Witherspoon. There is a Molly Pitcher Inn and a Molly Pitcher Exxon station in Monmouth County, and a Molly Pitcher

Moll Pitcher at Monmouth
This fanciful engraving has all the aspects of the legend: Molly Pitcher fires
the cannon at the British enemy, while at her feet are the water bucket
and her dead husband. Special Collections and University Archives, Rutgers
University Libraries—Women's Project of New Jersey Collection.

rest stop on the New Jersey Turnpike. Writers have hailed her as a pioneer American feminist. The Fisher-Price map of the United States, a toy that readers may remember from their childhood, depicts one famous person for each of the fifty states. The choice for New Jersey? Molly Pitcher, of course.

But for all her fame, we actually know quite little about the person called Molly Pitcher. She has much in common with figures like King Arthur, Robin Hood, and Davy Crockett—historical personages whose real lives have been usurped by myth. To isolate historical truth from quasi-historical legend, let us engage in some historical detective work to examine what has been written about Molly over the two and a quarter centuries since the battle of Monmouth. Like good detectives, we will sift the evidence and examine the reliability of the witnesses.

The Army Private and the Physician

At the battle of Monmouth on June 28, 1778, thirteen thousand American troops fought ten thousand British soldiers in the blistering heat of a Jersey summer. One of the Continental soldiers on the field that day was seventeen-year-old Joseph Plumb Martin, a private in a Connecticut regiment. More than half a century later, as an old man, Martin published a memoir of his Revolutionary War service, which included an account of "one little incident" he saw in the midst of the Monmouth conflict:

> A woman whose husband belonged to the artillery and who was then attached to a piece in the engagement, attended with her husband at the piece the whole time. While in the act of reaching a cartridge and having one of her feet as far before the other as she could step, a cannon shot from the enemy passed directly between her legs without doing any other damage than carrying away all the lower part of her petticoat. Looking at it with apparent unconcern, she observed that it was lucky it did not pass a little higher, for in that case it might have carried away something else, and continued her occupation.

This brief passage is a vitally important piece of evidence because it is the only first-person, eyewitness account relating to Molly from someone who was actually at the June 28 battle. But it is maddeningly devoid of detail—nowhere is the woman's name, or even the Molly Pitcher nick-name, used, and there are no supporting details about her husband or her husband's artillery unit. Moreover, the line about the petticoat sounds more like a soldier's smutty joke than an actual event. (Martin seems to have been fond of ribald humor—at another place in his memoir he makes wisecracks about the New Jersey town Maidenhead, now Lawrenceville.) The fact that Martin was writing five decades after the event raises questions about his reliability as a witness.

There is one account written less than a week after the battle that bears on the Molly Pitcher story, but this, too, is flawed, in this case because it is secondhand hearsay. The writer in question was Dr. Albigence Waldo, a physician with the Continental Army who, on July 3, 1778, wrote the following words in his diary:

> One of the camp women I must give a little praise to. Her gallant, whom she attended in battle, being shot down, she immediately took up his gun and cartridges and like a Spartan heroine fought with astonishing bravery, discharging the piece with as much regularity as any soldier present. This a wounded officer, whom I dressed [bandaged], told me he did see himself, she being in his platoon, and assured me I might depend on its truth.

Here again, there is no use of the Molly Pitcher nickname and no identifying information about the woman's identity or the identity of the wounded officer. One intriguing feature of Waldo's account is that the taking up of a gun and cartridges sounds more like shooting a musket than touching off an artillery piece. There is one other curiosity about the Waldo evidence. The lines above, from his diary, were quoted in a 1927 book on the Battle of Monmouth by William S. Stryker. In recent years historians intrigued by the Molly Pitcher story have attempted to find the original document, but so far without success. Stryker was a respected researcher whose work is still considered reliable, but the inability to find the original source raises a nagging doubt.

A Legend Is Born

The evidence of Private Martin and Physician Waldo is thin indeed. But beginning in the late 1830s, a legend emerged about the heroine of Monmouth, with extravagant details about her battlefield accomplishments. The earliest surviving written version of the legend is a brief article that appeared in the December 1, 1837, *New-Jersey State Gazette*, evidently reprinted from an article published not long before in the *New Brunswick Times*:

MOLLY PITCHER.—For the benefit of that class of full grown children and embryo patriots, who talk much more of New Jersey chivalry about election times than they ever learned, or [are] likely to learn from history, it may be proper here to add—what every New Jersey boy should know—that at the commencement of the battle of Monmouth this intrepid woman contributed her aid by constantly carrying water from a spring to the battery, where her husband was employed, as a cannonier, in loading and firing a gun. At length he was shot dead in her presence, just as she was leaving the spring; whereupon she flew to the spot—found her husband lifeless, and, at the moment, heard an officer, who rode up, order off the gun "for want of a man sufficiently dauntless to supply his place." Indignant at this order, and stung by the remark, she promptly opposed it—demanded the post of her slain husband to avenge his death—flew to the gun, and, to the admiration and astonishment of all who saw her, assumed and ably discharged the duties of the thus vacated post of cannonier, to the end of the battle! For this sterling demonstration of genuine **WHIG** spirit, Washington gave her a lieutenant's commission upon the spot, which congress afterwards ratified. And granted her a sword, and an epaulette, and half pay, as a lieutenant, for life! She wore the epaulette, received the pay, and was called "Captain Molly!" ever afterwards.   —*N.B. Times.*

Where did the elements of this article come from? Was it an oral tradition that had circulated in New Jersey since the Revolution? Was it a flight of some unknown newspaper editor's fancy, perhaps inspired by the publication in 1830 of Private Joseph Plumb Martin's brief but suggestive paragraph in his wartime memoir? Or more likely, was it some combination of local tradition elaborated by literary imagination?

Deepening the mystery is the pension application of Rebecca Clendenen. After the American Revolution, veterans and their widows were entitled to receive a pension from the federal government. Because military personnel records from the war were scanty, pension applicants were encouraged to provide as much detail as possible to back up their claim of military service. In her 1840 application, filed three years after the *Gazette* article appeared, Rebecca Clendenen, widow of a Pennsylvania veteran, stated that she had often heard her husband speak of the Battle of Monmouth, where "a woman who was called by the troops Captain Molly was busily engaged in carrying canteens of water to the famished soldiers." Was the widow's recollection of her husband's recollection accurate, or was she (or some professional pension-application writer) borrowing from the legend that was by now appearing in print?

"Them Redcoats, Bad Luck to Them"

Whatever it was true or false, the Molly story had legs. This was the era when the nation was being torn by disunion that would ultimately lead to civil war. Like our own admiration for the "greatest generation" of World War II, there was nostalgia for the heroes of the Revolutionary War era. Molly Pitcher filled that need. In February 1840, the article "Recollections and Private Memoirs of the Life and Character of Washington" by George Washington Parke Custis appeared in the *Washington National Intelligencer*. Custis, who was the adopted son of Washington, added new details to the story of Molly Pitcher. The Molly legend surfaced thereafter in other works, such as the *Historical Collections of the State of New Jersey* by John W. Barber and Henry Howe (1844) and *Pictorial Field-Book of the Revolution* by Benson J. Lossing (1851). It continued long after the Civil War and well into the twentieth century in books, magazine articles, and school texts. A monument to Molly Pitcher was erected in Pennsylvania on July 4, 1876, the centennial of the nation's birth, perhaps symbolizing the entry of Molly Pitcher at Monmouth into the pantheon of patriotic icons that includes Washington at Valley Forge, the Minutemen at Lexington, and the signing of the Declaration of Independence in Philadelphia.

Let us summarize this canonical (pun intended) Molly legend. In most versions prior to around 1860, the heroine of Monmouth was referred to as Captain Molly, but in later versions, more commonly as Molly Pitcher. She is depicted as an army camp follower who carried water to thirsty soldiers at the Battle of Monmouth. When her artilleryman husband falls dead (or in some versions is wounded or overcome by heat), she takes his place at the cannon. For this feat, she becomes the toast of the army, saluted by Generals Greene and Lafayette, and familiarly chatted up by the mighty Washington. She receives money in the form of coin or a pension, and is awarded an honorary commission as a sergeant, lieutenant, or captain, depending on the version. In some accounts, she fashions a crude sort of uniform of military jacket and petticoats, topped by a cocked hat. In some, she receives a sword, while in others she speaks in elevated language, such as: "Since my brave husband is no more I will use my utmost exertions to avenge his death." In other versions, she speaks in a vaudeville Irish accent, yearning "for another clap at them redcoats, bad luck to them."

A typical example of this melodramatic version of the Molly Pitcher story comes in a 1905 article in *American Monthly Magazine* by Isabella Crater McGeorge:

> . . . Washington praised [Molly] and conferred the brevet of captain on her, hence her title, Captain Molly. He also said that she should have half-pay for life. Then the grand French officer General Lafayette, asked that his men "might have the pleasure of giving madam a trifle." Although there were no French troops on the field at that date, yet there were many French officers who had volunteered in American regiments. The Frenchmen are ever appreciative of heroines who have worsted the English and they showered their extra silver upon the "brave Marie"—the trifle proving to be a hatful of coin.

A poem (albeit a dreadful one) by nineteenth-century poet Thomas Dunn English paints a dramatic picture of Molly at the battle:

As we turned our flanks and center in the path of death to enter,
  One of Knox's brass six-pounders lost its Irish cannoneer,
And his wife who 'mid the slaughter had been bearing pails of water
  For the gun and for the gunners, over his body shed a tear.
'Move the piece;' but there they found her, loading, firing that six-pounder,
  And she bravely, 'til we won, worked the gun.

Molly appeared in pictorial form as well as in rhyme. One of the first illustrations was a painting by George Washington Parke Custis, done sometime in the period 1840–1850. An engraved version of the Custis painting appeared in Lossing's *Pictorial Field Book* in 1851. An 1848 painting by Nathaniel Currier was translated into a series of popular Currier & Ives prints. Countless other images of Molly have appeared over the years, including a label on barrels of cranberries shipped from New Jersey. All of these illustrations depict a gritty, resolute Molly at the cannon.

The power of this legend was so strong that it led to attempts to find the well where Molly Pitcher supposedly drew water for the troops. In the early twentieth century, officials of the Pennsylvania Railroad put up signs next to an old well located near the tracks that ran at the edge of the battlefield. The purpose may have been to give tourists something to look at and to keep curiosity seekers from injuring themselves by crossing the rail line to look for Molly's well elsewhere on the battlefield. Local farmers claimed at least three conflicting locations for the well, and in the 1930s local historians walked the battlefield with divining rods in order to try to find Molly's source of water. There are presently two signs on the battlefield claiming to mark the site of Molly's well (a third marker has disappeared), but none of them appears to have any foundation in fact. If there was a source of water used by Molly, the best evidence, linked with the location where Joseph Plumb Martin and Mrs. Clendenen's husband fought, suggests that it was a spring (not a well) located behind Perrine Ridge on the northwestern side of the battlefield.

The Widow Hamilton Speaks

We have used the term "legend" in describing the picture of Molly Pitcher that emerged in the late 1830s and has persisted into our own day, a legend that soars far above the thin primary sources. But there exists testimony from one person who was in a position to know the truth—the aged widow of Alexander Hamilton, Elizabeth Schuyler Hamilton. If true, Mrs. Hamilton's testimony provides a factual underpinning to the legend. Alexander Hamilton was at the Battle of Monmouth in 1778 as an aide to General Washington. He died in 1804 in his infamous duel with Aaron Burr. His wife, Elizabeth, survived him by a half century. In 1848, when Mrs. Hamilton was ninety-two, she was interviewed in her home by historian and artist Benson J. Lossing. At his prompting, she reminisced about the dramatic days of the Revolution. "Who was Captain Molly, and for what was she famous?" asked Lossing in the course of their conversation. "Why, don't you remember reading of her exploit at the battle of Monmouth?" replied the widow, who proceeded to relate the story of the woman who brought water to the soldiers at Monmouth, took her dead husband's place at the cannon, wore a uniform that combined petticoats, military jacket, and cocked hat, received a sergeant's commission from General Washington, a half-pay pension, and showers of coins from the French. Widow Hamilton said she had met Captain Molly on several occasions.

What to make of this? By the year 1848, the legend of Molly Pitcher was well advanced, and the widow Hamilton's remarks, perhaps urged on by Lossing, were similar to versions already in print. These days our memories of the past that we lived through are powerfully shaped by Hollywood. Mass media was still in its infancy in 1848, but it may well have influenced the aged widow Hamilton's recollections.

One aspect of her testimony that shows her confusion about the past—a confusion shared by many others before and since—is the conflation of Molly Pitcher with Molly Corbin. Unlike Molly Pitcher, the story of Margaret "Molly" Corbin (1751–1800) is well documented. During the battle of Fort Washington, New York, on November 16, 1776, an American artilleryman was mortally wounded, and his wife, Margaret, took his place at the cannon. She, too, was severely wounded, but she survived, and in gratitude for her sacrifice, Congress voted her half pay for life. She was well known as "Captain Molly" after the war, but died broken-down and poor near West Point, where she is now buried. Her act of bravery as a female firing a cannon in place of her fallen husband, as well as her name ("Molly") and nickname ("Captain Molly") were so similar to those of Molly Pitcher of Monmouth fame that their two stories became utterly intermingled and it is now very difficult to disentangle them.

Meanwhile, Back in Carlisle

We now need to shift our attention to Carlisle, Pennsylvania, where in the late eighteenth and early nineteenth century lived one Mary Hays

McCauley, variously spelled McKolly, McAuley, Mcauley, McCauly, McCally, McCalla, and sometimes referred to by the first name Molly or Polly, both of which are familiar forms of the name Mary. As evidenced by legal documents she signed with an "X," she was illiterate.

Researchers have found that she had been married to a William Hays, who was listed on the Carlisle tax rolls as a barber. The tax records suggest that William and Mary arrived in Carlisle in 1783. William died there in 1787, leaving Mary as a widow with a five-year-old son, John Hays. Mary subsequently married John McCauley, who died around 1813. The widow eventually moved in with her son, who was by now grown up. She died in 1832.

A very strong case can be made that Mary McCauley was Molly Pitcher. In 1822 the Pennsylvania legislature, at her request, awarded her a pension. When the bill was introduced in the legislature, it justified the pension on the grounds that she was the "widow of a soldier of the revolutionary war." But the bill's text was subsequently changed to award the pension "for her services during the revolutionary war." It was quite unusual for a woman to receive a pension for her own war record, rather than simply as a surviving spouse of a veteran. In fact the only other woman known to have received a pension for her own actions during the Revolution was Margaret Corbin, who was wounded in action at Fort Washington. News of McCauley's pension appeared in newspapers in New York, Philadelphia, and Washington, but nowhere did it use the term Molly Pitcher or speak of the Battle of Monmouth.

Now comes the clincher. Mary's first husband, William Hays, served with Colonel John Proctor's Pennsylvania Regiment of Artillery, which fought at the Battle of Monmouth. He was discharged from service in 1783, the exact year when William and Mary show up in the Carlisle tax records.

On January 26, 1832, the *Carlisle Herald* published Mary's obituary:

DIED on Sunday last, Mrs. MARY MCAULEY, aged about 90 years. The history of this woman is somewhat remarkable. Her first husband's name was Hays, who was a soldier in the war of the Revolution. It appears that she continued with him while in the army, and acted so much the part of the heroine, as to attract the notice of the officers. Some estimate may be found of the value of the service rendered by her, when the fact is stated, that she drew a pension from [the] government during the latter years of her life.

If the *Herald*'s information is correct, she would have been about thirty-six at the time of the Battle of Monmouth. But a monument erected to her memory a half century after she died gives her age at death as seventy-nine, which would have made her around twenty-five in the year of the Battle of Monmouth. The latter date is more consistent with census records. We do not know her maiden name or her family background. A commonly held belief is that she was of German origin, born as Mary Ludwig. However, this identification is based on the false belief that Mary McCauley was married to a man named John Casper Hays from Carlisle, not William Hays. Another mid-nineteenth-century source claims that Molly was one Mary Hanna from Mercer County, New Jersey, but there is no primary evidence to support this claim. The weight of evidence suggests that she was of Irish origin, not German or English, particularly since her first husband, William Hays, was said to be an Irish immigrant.

What was she like in real life? In the late nineteenth century several elderly Pennsylvanians claimed that, as children in Carlisle, they had known Mary McCauley. They recalled her as a talkative old woman who, although "rough and uncouth in her expressions," was eager to describe her Revolutionary War experiences as Molly Pitcher. Mrs. Susan Heckendorn remembered, "She often told this deponent and her girl friends the story of her army life, and her experience at the Battle of Monmouth, and said to them, 'You girls should have been with me at the Battle of Monmouth and learned how to load a cannon.'" Physically she was remembered as homely, short, and stout, with hairy bristles coming out of her nose and a defective eye—not quite the romantic Hollywood image of a battlefield action heroine.

It is hard to say how much of these recollections were tainted by the popular legend of Molly that had emerged in the late 1830s, and by the fact that the recollectors were trying to remember episodes from their long-ago childhoods. For example, the memoirs repeat the old story that

Molly's husband died in the battle—yet he seems to have been very much alive after the war when he was clipping hair in Carlisle.

————

So what is true and what is false in the Molly Pitcher saga? The elaborations of the story that began in the late 1830s, with the flowery language, the comic uniform, the relationship with Washington, and the whole panoply of swords, pensions, cockades, and battlefield wells are false, or at the least widely exaggerated. Molly's alleged recognition by the senior commanders of the Continental Army is nowhere mentioned in the voluminous correspondence of George Washington or other military and political figures of the period. But this does not negate the testimony of Private Martin and Dr. Waldo, along with the action of the Pennsylvania legislature. The evidence is persuasive that there really was a woman at the Battle of Monmouth who performed heroically and that this woman was Mary McCauley—even though she may never in her life have heard the name "Molly Pitcher."

There is enough in this story to warrant our admiration for this illiterate camp follower who, in a moment of crisis, proved that military bravery is a quality that is not confined to the male sex.

6 The Caldwell Murder Case

In June 1780, a Revolutionary War battle took place in Connecticut Farms (now Union Township), New Jersey, when American Continental troops and militia clashed with a British and Hessian invading force.

A group of women and children took refuge in the bedroom of a house to escape the battle. Suddenly a musket ball came smashing through the window, killing one of the women, who was sitting on the bed comforting her frightened children. The other women fled, taking the children with them. The house, with the corpse still lying on the bed, was later burned by British looters.

The dead woman was Hannah Caldwell, wife of the Reverend James Caldwell, minister of the Presbyterian church in Elizabethtown. The Reverend Caldwell was an early enthusiast of independence from Britain; when the war broke out he had donned a uniform and joined the Continental Army, first as a chaplain and later as deputy quartermaster.

The grieving Reverend Caldwell was convinced that the death of his wife had not been an accident. He believed that she had been killed on orders of the British high command, under the influence of the Tories seeking revenge for their exile from Elizabethtown.

As proof, Caldwell pointed to the fact that the window faced away from the battle that was being fought a half mile from the house. A village girl who had been in the room at the time stated that she had seen from the window a red-coated British soldier approach the house and take deliberate aim with his musket. Caldwell said that British officers had later been overheard talking of the death in a manner suggesting it had been ordered by their superiors.

Caldwell published his charges in a pamphlet entitled *Certain Facts Relating to the Tragic Death of Hannah Caldwell,* and the story became a staple of American atrocity charges against the British.

Then came a tragic postscript. A year and a half after the death of his wife, the Reverend Caldwell was shot to death by an American sentry as the minister walked along the Elizabethtown waterfront. It was believed that the sentry had been paid by the Tories to commit the murder, and the man was hanged.

The story of the Caldwell murders became a tradition in New Jersey after the Revolution; parents taught their children how the fighting parson and his gentle wife were martyrs to the patriot cause. An engraving of Mrs. Caldwell being shot dead by the British soldier still adorns the official seal of Union County.

One of the elements grafted onto the tale was a sort of ghost story. It was said that in the midst of a thunderstorm, the night after Mrs.

Caldwell was killed, a gang of British soldiers broke into an Elizabethtown mansion. A flash of lightening suddenly illuminated a woman of the household dressed in white descending the stairs. One of the British soldiers was supposed to have exclaimed in horror (but without forgetting his grammar) "My God! Mrs. Caldwell whom we killed today."

But a half century later, one William C. DeHart dared to question the entire tradition of the Caldwell murders. DeHart was an Elizabethtown native who had gone off to serve in the U.S. Army on the Mexican border. He had contracted some unknown illness (probably chronic dysentery) during his service and had been invalided back home on a pension.

He arrived in Elizabethtown just about the time a monument to the Reverend Caldwell was unveiled in the town. It was the occasion for great patriotic speeches about the martyred couple. But something about the tale struck Captain DeHart as fishy. He did some research by talking to elderly residents and examining old military records.

In February 1846 he published an article in the *Newark Daily Advertiser* in which he speculated that Hannah Caldwell might have been killed by a stray bullet from the battle or perhaps murdered by a disgruntled former employee of the family. He flatly rejected the old tradition that she had been deliberately marked for death on the order of the enemy commander, and he scoffed at the ghost story as inherently improbable.

Captain DeHart also denied the traditional story of the Reverend Caldwell's death. He said that the sentry had been posted to prevent smuggling and had seen Caldwell remove a package from a British ship that had docked in Elizabethtown under a flag of truce. The sentry commanded the minister to put down the package; when Caldwell refused, the sentry fired his musket. The sentry was guilty of overzealousness, said DeHart, but not of deliberate murder. If the sentry had been hired to kill Caldwell, asked DeHart, why would he choose to commit the crime on "a public occasion, in open day, in the presence of numerous bystanders, and with the certainty of apprehension?"

DeHart's article shocked the historical establishment of Elizabethtown and, in particular, the Reverend Nicholas Murray, who was the town's unofficial historian and the minister of the same Presbyterian church where Caldwell had once served.

An angry exchange of letters between Captain DeHart and Reverend Murray ensued in the pages of the *Daily Advertiser*—the same kind of nasty backbiting you can see these days in the letters page of book-review journals.

Murray attacked DeHart mostly on the grounds that the canonical story that the Caldwells had been murdered had to be true because it had always been thought so and because to think otherwise would be to diminish the fame of the heroic Reverend Caldwell and to excuse the hated Tories who had burned and pillaged New Jersey. Murray pointed out that DeHart was an Episcopalian, and so it was natural that he would defend the Tory Church of England position and vilify Elizabethtown's Presbyterian patriots.

DeHart delivered a low ball of his own. He informed his readers that Murray had been born in Ireland, a fact in the 1840s so damning that no further explanation was needed. But for the most part, DeHart was much less dogmatic, much more flexible than Murray. He did not present his findings as absolute truth, but as a hypothesis, and said that if his opponents could present better evidence, he would gladly revise his opinion.

The debate did not last very long. Captain DeHart died of his Mexican ailment in 1848, at age forty-eight, two years after his article was published.

So was the death of the Caldwells a sinister conspiracy, or simply an accident of war caused by wartime stupidity? We will never know for certain the answer to this whodunit, but the approach of Captain DeHart certainly seems more persuasive. As an army veteran, he seems to have known that where there are armed men shooting at each other, innocent people become casualties, as we have learned by watching the news from the Middle East, and, alas, inner-city America.

In the case of Mrs. Caldwell, it is not hard to imagine a nervous British soldier stationed on the flank of the battle who sees a shadow at the window and, thinking it a sniper, raises his musket and fires. And it is a coincidence, but only a coincidence, that a similar fate befell the Reverend Caldwell when a nervous sentry fired at a man behaving suspiciously.

When faced with a choice between conspiracy and stupidity in human affairs, go with stupidity every time.

7   "The Cow Chace"

Why did the British lose the American Revolution? There are all sorts of convoluted explanations about the length of supply lines across the Atlantic, eighteenth-century infantry tactics, British colonial policy, and so forth. But maybe the saga of the Cow Chase tells it all.

The story begins with a rebel blunder in New Jersey. On July 21, 1780, American General Anthony Wayne led a force of a thousand Continental soldiers and militia along the palisades overlooking the Hudson River to an isolated spot known as Bull's Ferry (now part of Hackensack). Their objective was to capture a blockhouse used by Tories as a base for terrorizing American settlements in the area.

The blockhouse was formidable. It was built of stout logs at the top of a bluff and protected by fortifications and cannon. The Americans fired on the blockhouse with artillery and muskets, but to no effect. When they charged the fortress, they were driven back by the defender's gunfire. Wayne decided to call off the attack; twenty of his men had been killed and forty-six wounded. He feared that British regulars from Manhattan would cross the Hudson to counterattack. As he retreated, he drove off the Tories' cattle and burned their boats.

The affair at Bull's Ferry was an embarrassment for the American side, particularly since it turned out there had been a mere eighty-four Tories inside the blockhouse. The British trumpeted the event as if it had been a great battlefield triumph. King George III himself sent congratu-

Capture of André
In this Currier & Ives image, British Major John André is captured near
Tarrytown, New York, on September 23, 1780, by rebel militiamen, who
find the plans for West Point hidden in his stocking. A few months before
his capture he had mocked the American military with a poem written
about a battle in New Jersey. Library of Congress.

lations to the Tory defenders of the blockhouse, who had defeated a force
ten times their size.

The British glee was understandable. After six years of bitter warfare,
King George and his armies had been unable to snuff out the rebellion.
The British were cooped up in New York City, while the rebels controlled
the countryside. Public opinion back home in England was becoming
disgusted with the unending war. For British officers stationed in Manhattan, the affair at Bull's Ferry was a welcome victory.

One of those officers was thirty-year-old Major John André, an
aide to General Sir Henry Clinton. André, the son of a well-to-do London merchant family, was an aspiring aristocrat. His experience in
America had taught him to despise the rebels as a threat to the natural
rule of the better sort over the mob. He had participated in military
campaigns against New Jersey and was present at a gory episode in 1778

when the British bayoneted American soldiers as they slept or tried to surrender.

André was talented, and he loved to entertain his fellow officers and their coterie of Tory hangers-on, particularly refined young ladies, with poetry readings, musical recitals, and amateur theatricals. To celebrate the Bull's Ferry victory in New Jersey, he composed a long mock-epic poem, which he contributed in installments to the New York Tory newspaper, *The Gazette*. André entitled his poem "The Cow Chase" (or in eighteenth-century spelling, "The Cow Chace"). The work was a parody of "Chevy Chase," a popular English ballad from the Middle Ages.

In his poem, André lampooned the American officers as drunkards and simpletons. He pictured General Wayne imbibing corn whisky and wearing crude clothing. He made fun of the fact that in civilian life Wayne had been a tanner, and how at the battle of the blockhouse, it was Wayne's hide that had gotten tanned.

André also poked fun at the undisciplined American peasants, men with absurd names like Thaddeus Posset, Titus Hooper, Nathan Pumpkin, and Yan Van Poop. He laughed at their tattered appearance and poor training, and at how they worked up their courage before the battle:

> Then from the cask of rum once more
>   They took a heady gill;
> When, one and all, they loudly swore
>   They'd fight upon the hill.

André described how the Americans broke ranks and ran away, stopping only to steal livestock. He depicted the cloud of dust raised by the stampede of stolen cows, sheep, horses, goats, and chickens, and how American General Light Horse Harry Lee brought up the rear:

> Sublime upon his stirrups rose
>   The mighty Lee behind,
> And drove the terror-smitten cows
>   Like chaff before the wind.

There was a bedrock of bitterness underneath the mocking tone of André's poem. He described the Americans as "dung-born," and argued that soldiers of this peasant army deserved hanging for their "curs'd rebellion."

André ended the poem with pretended terror at being someday captured by the enemy:

And now I've closed my epic strain,
    I tremble as I shew it;
Lest this same warrio-drover Wayne
    Should ever catch the poet!

"The Cow Chace" might well have been forgotten as a minor, and not very successful, effort at parody, just one more example of how people in wartime tend to belittle the enemy. But what makes this poem memorable is the fate that ultimately befell its author.

Not long after completing his poem, André was sent on an important secret mission. Word had reached the British that one of the Continental Army's highest officers, General Benedict Arnold, was willing to turn traitor. By night, André was ferried from the British warship *Vulture* to a point along the Hudson where he met Arnold.

Together Arnold and André conceived a bold plot. The British would launch a prearranged attack on the fortress at West Point, which Arnold commanded. The turncoat Arnold would then surrender the fort and its three thousand defenders. It was to be a great victory for the British and a killing blow to the American cause. In exchange, Arnold was to receive ten thousand pounds and a commission in the king's army.

When the time came for André to return to the British lines, he took off his uniform and disguised himself as a civilian merchant with the assumed name "John Anderson." In his pocket was a pass signed by Arnold; hidden in one of his stockings was the plan for the defense of West Point.

As he rode along toward safety, André no doubt took pride that he was playing a key role in the defeat of the rebellion. But just then he was stopped by three rebel militiamen. The three were exactly the sort of crude peasants in ragged uniforms he had lampooned in his poem: one even had the ludicrous name Isaac Van Wart. André casually showed them his pass from Arnold.

But these Americans were smart enough to realize that André was up to no good; they stripped him naked and found the secret paper hidden in his stocking. André was delivered as a prisoner to the American army. The prediction he had written in "The Cow Chace" of being captured by the rebels had come true.

When he heard of André's capture, Benedict Arnold fled to Manhattan. The plan to surrender West Point was aborted.

Because he had been caught while wearing civilian clothes, André was convicted of spying and sentenced to death. Writing as one gentleman to another, he requested of General Washington that he be shot by a firing squad, rather than hanged like a felon. But the stern Washington refused.

André was brought to the gallows in Tappan, New York, on October 2, 1780. As the rope was placed about his neck, it may have occurred to his cultured mind that he had underestimated this nation of uppity peasants.

8  Classical Gas

This is a story about a pioneering scientific experiment in an unlikely place with a celebrity cast.

In the closing days of the American Revolution, in August of 1783, the commander in chief of the American army, General George Washington, established his headquarters at Rocky Hill, New Jersey, in order to be close to the Congress, which was in session at nearby Princeton. The house, known as Rockingham, has been restored to the way it looked when Washington was in residence and is today a historic site open to the public.

After seven brutal years of war, peace had finally been won, and Washington had the luxury of chatting with comrades who had been part of that great struggle and had journeyed to see him at Rockingham. One of those friends was Thomas Paine, who Washington invited to pay a visit.

Thomas Paine
Along with General George Washington, the British-born Paine, a
pamphleteer during the Revolutionary War era, carried out a scientific
experiment on the Millstone River in 1783. Library of Congress.

Paine was the man who had written two powerful pamphlets—*Common Sense* and *The Crisis*—that rallied Americans to the cause of independence and liberty. Paine had also served as a soldier in Washington's army in the darkest days of the conflict. The British-born Paine was a fiery atheist and radical, quite different in temperament from Washington, the aloof Virginia aristocrat, yet the two had developed a bond of friendship from their war years.

During his visit to Rockingham, Paine got into a debate with Washington and some of his officers about the curious fact that the Millstone

River, which ran its sluggish course past Rockingham, could be set on fire. Two officers on Washington's staff argued that the phenomenon must be caused by combustible solid material that rose from the river bottom. But Paine thought the cause was what he called "inflammable air"—in other words, some kind of swamp gas.

It is striking that Washington and his officers, military men all, would get caught up in a serious discussion with the political pamphleteer Paine about science. But this was the glorious Age of Enlightenment, when reason and rationality were in the air. Since it was a time when people were confident that they could discover truth for themselves and need not blindly accept dogma, the group decided to put their competing theories to the test. The next evening Paine, Washington, and some officers and soldiers boarded a flat-bottomed boat on the river. They chose to do this at night so that any fire that arose in the course of their experiment would be more visible. The date was November 5, 1783. It may have been the first scientific experiment conducted in the new American nation created by the Declaration of Independence.

The soldiers stirred up muck at the bottom of the river with poles, while Paine and Washington leaned over the side of the scow with burning paper in their hands a few inches above the water's surface. According to Paine, "When the mud at the bottom was disturbed by the poles, the air bubbles rose fast, and I saw the fire take from General Washington's light and descend from thence to the surface of the water." This was, he said, "demonstrative evidence that what was called setting the river on fire was setting on fire the inflammable air that arose out of the mud." Neither Paine nor Washington knew it, but the gas they ignited was methane. A scientist in Italy, Alessandro Giuseppe Antonio Anastasio Volta, had experimented with the gas in 1776, but with the slowness of communication across the Atlantic in that war-ravaged era, the news does not seem to have reached Washington, Paine, or their contemporaries in the New World. (Volta, by the way, was a pioneer in the field of electricity, and the unit of electrical energy we know as the volt was named in his honor.)

What exactly is methane? As Paine guessed, it can be formed from rotting organic matter, like decomposing gunk at the bottom of rivers and lakes. (Cow belches and farts are also a major source, and even you and I, dear reader, can be considered methane-producing machines.) Methane has been identified as a greenhouse gas that is now increasing rapidly in the atmosphere, and in the opinion of scientists is contributing to global warming.

After the experiment at Rockingham, the two principals in this story went their separate ways. Washington became the chair of the Constitutional Convention and first president of the United States. Paine journeyed to Europe to continue his career as a radical. He wrote the incendiary, free-thinking book *Rights of Man*, which he dedicated to Washington. During the tumultuous French Revolution, a much messier affair than the American version, Paine spent some time in a Paris prison and narrowly avoided being guillotined.

A postscript: A group of microbiologists at Rutgers—Douglas E. Eveleigh, Craig Phillips, and Lilly Young—have become fascinated by the Rockingham story. They bring students to murky, muddy watering holes where they together re-create the Paine–Washington experiment. The fact that the father of our country forthrightly engaged in hands-on science, the professors feel, is a worthwhile lesson to disseminate to Americans in our age, when pseudo science and superstition are crowding out the rationalist legacy of the Enlightenment. Hats off to the Rutgers methane igniters!

9  The Congressman's Cold

The French philosopher Pascal observed that if Cleopatra's nose had been an inch longer the history of the world would have been utterly different. What Pascal was saying (apart from the fact that he found short noses sexy) was that great events are determined by small things.

John Beatty
Because of a cold, this New Jersey delegate to the Congress of the
new nation missed an all-important vote on the abolition of slavery.
Special Collections and University Archives, Rutgers University Libraries—
New Jersey Portraits Collection.

An example from American history: If a New Jersey congressman
had not caught cold, slavery might have been abolished and the Civil War
might never have been fought. Well, maybe.

The year was 1784 and the American Revolution had ended in victory
the year before. The new nation now had to ponder how to govern itself.
One problem was the millions of acres of territory that stretched west of
the original thirteen colonies to the Mississippi. Should this land be kept
as subordinate colonies or organized into new states?

Thomas Jefferson was a delegate to Congress from Virginia. Eight years before, he had written the Declaration of Independence; now he applied his fine Enlightenment mind to the issue of the territories. Working with a congressional committee he devised a plan that would allow the settlers in these lands to elect representatives and draft laws, and then to create states that would be admitted to the Union. He even invented the names of the new states—such as Michigania, Cheronesus, Assinispia, and Pelisipia.

And in a departure from the history of the world, Jefferson and the committee put down on paper the principle that the new territory was not to be treated as a colony for the mother country to exploit, but rather as an equal partner with the existing states of the Union.

Jefferson's proposed ordinance contained an explosive clause affecting the territories: "After the year 1800 of the Christian era, there shall be neither slavery nor involuntary servitude." This proposal was particularly significant because it applied not only to the territory then available north of the Ohio River, but also with other land in the South that might later be acquired by the government.

It was a pivotal moment in American history. Sentiment was growing in the North that slavery should be abolished, and emancipation laws were moving through state legislatures. Even some Southerners thought the time had come to end slavery. The cotton gin, which would make slavery economically feasible in the South, had not yet entered the mind of Eli Whitney.

The subject of Jefferson and slavery is an intriguing one. He himself kept slaves, but at the same time hated the institution and hoped for its abolition. And it is now almost certain that starting in the late 1780s he had a slave mistress.

Jefferson's proposed legislation came before Congress in sections. The proposal for organizing the states was widely supported, but the abolition clause was not. It called forth opposition from many Southerners, who, reacting against pressure from Northerners, were beginning to see slavery not as a necessary evil but as a positive good.

The matter came to a vote on April 19, 1784. In those days, ballots in Congress were cast by states—a majority of each state's congressional delegation determined whether the state's vote was yea or nay.

Jefferson needed seven states (a majority of the thirteen). He quickly lost the South; except for Jefferson and one North Carolina congressman, every Southerner voted against the measure. The six states from Pennsylvania northward went solidly for it. New Jersey held the balance: a positive vote would give Jefferson his seventh state and victory.

But that never happened. One New Jersey congressman who favored the abolition clause, John Beatty, had a cold and stayed in his lodgings that day. As a result, New Jersey did not have the requisite minimum of at least two members present to cast a vote. The Southern states, with a minority of the population, won a victory.

You could make a case that had Beatty managed to come to Congress that day, slavery would never have existed in the Southern states that were eventually added to the Union, including Alabama, Louisiana, and Mississippi. The peculiar institution would have been isolated in the states of the Old South along the Atlantic, where it would have withered away.

If that had happened, then perhaps the bloodbath of the Civil War would never have occurred. Perhaps racial relations in the United States might have been less turbulent and the division between North and South less profound.

Jefferson saw it that way. He wrote to a friend in France about the disaster caused by the Jersey delegate's absence from Congress: "The voice of a single individual would have prevented this abominable crime from spreading itself over the new country. Thus we see the fate of millions of unborn hanging on the tongue of one man, and Heaven was silent in that awful moment." In later years he wrote of the irony that a people who had fought for their own liberty during the American Revolution could blithely oppress their fellow men with whipping, starvation, and death. "What a stupendous, what an incomprehensible machine is man!" Jefferson lamented.

Who was Congressman John Beatty of New Jersey? He certainly had a killer resumé: graduate of Princeton, practicing lawyer and physician, colonel in Washington's army during the Revolution, founder of the New Jersey Medical Society, president of the Trenton Banking Company, speaker of the New Jersey General Assembly, brigadier general in the New Jersey militia, member of the U.S. House of Representatives, prominent Mason, powerhouse in the state Federalist Party.

His cold came in the midst of this impressive career; if he felt remorse about missing a crucial vote, no evidence of it survives.

There was one other skeleton in Beatty's closet. It seems that during the Revolution, General Washington placed him in charge of all captured British and Hessian prisoners. (The fact that Beatty had been a prisoner of war in British hands for a year and a half qualified him for the post.) But it came out that as commissioner of prisoners, Beatty was trading with the enemy. He was court martialed and given a public reprimand by Washington, who described his behavior as "extremely reprehensible." Whereupon Beatty resigned from the army.

The episode didn't seem to bother Beatty overmuch or hinder his career. He was a political supporter of Washington, and as Speaker of the Assembly, welcomed the father of his country to New Jersey.

Was Beatty's absence from Congress really so pivotal? Probably not. It is unlikely that the South would ever have given up slavery so easily, and if the measure passed it would undoubtedly come up for a vote again. Indeed, Jefferson's 1784 ordinance was amended in fundamental ways by later congressional legislation.

But you never know. The late Harvard biologist Stephen Jay Gould spoke of the importance of contingency in the natural history of our planet. Change one event in a long sequence, he said, and the outcome will be different. Nothing is predetermined, nothing is inevitable. If the Earth had not been struck by an object from outer space sixty-five million years ago, dinosaurs might not have become extinct and the human species might never have evolved.

Cleopatra's nose, dinosaurs, and John Beatty's cold—it's an uncertain world out there.

10 The First Flight

On January 9, 1793, Monsieur Jean Pierre Blanchard traveled from Philadelphia across the Delaware River to New Jersey, accompanied by a little dog. What made his trip worthy of remembering is that he did it 5,812 feet in the air. It was the first human flight in the Western Hemisphere, 110 years before the Wright brothers.

Balloons are sort of ho-hum in this age of space travel, but back in the eighteenth century, lighter-than-air flight was a giant step for mankind. For the first time in history, humans could leave the surface of the earth to soar over church steeples and hills.

Aerial balloons were invented by the Montgolfier brothers of France in the early 1780s. The first flights produced excitement and astonishment. When one balloon came down in a French village, frightened peasants thought the moon had fallen from the sky.

It took some time before anyone dared to send up a balloon with a human passenger, since there was considerable doubt that anyone could breathe at that height. In a bold experiment, a balloon was launched in Paris with a duck, a sheep, and a rooster on board. Spectators were delighted when they found that the animals were still alive when the balloon came down.

A few weeks later a man went up in a balloon that was tethered to the ground with a rope. A short time after that, two Frenchmen made a free flight. Before long, bold aeronauts were making flights all over Europe.

Those pioneer balloonists were daredevils, much like the barnstormers of the early airplane age, making a living by wowing the astonished yokels. It was a perilous business; the early balloons had a habit of colliding with buildings, trees, and the ground. Hydrogen balloons exploded; hot-air balloons caught fire. The only thing the balloonist could control was going up and coming back down; the direction was determined by the whim of the winds.

One of the first of the European aeronauts was the Frenchman Jean Pierre Blanchard. A portrait shows him as a small man with a massive head, rather like a balloon. He was a hot-tempered and proud character, but he was undeniably brave.

Blanchard's best-known accomplishment was the first-ever flight across the English Channel, which he made in 1785. He and his companion

Jean Pierre Blanchard
The daring French aviation pioneer made the first balloon flight in the western hemisphere, from Philadelphia to Deptford, in 1793. Special Collections and University Archives, Rutgers University Libraries—Pictorial Collection.

JEAN PIERRE   BLANCHARD.

on that trip took off from the English side of the channel. The balloon began to sink over the ocean, and to keep from ditching, they had to throw everything overboard, including their trousers and coats and even their urine. After three hours they managed to come to a safe landing in France, freezing and nearly naked.

His channel crossing made Blanchard a celebrity. But while he had achieved fame, he was unable to amass much money from his flights. His temper was also getting him in trouble, and on one occasion he was thrown into an Austrian jail as an agent of the French Revolution. In 1792 Blanchard packed his balloon and his family on board ship and sailed to Philadelphia, the capital of the United States, to find a new audience.

Americans had been fascinated by the eyewitness accounts of balloon ascensions sent back from France by Benjamin Franklin, Thomas Jefferson, and other overseas compatriots. In Baltimore a man had gone aloft in a tethered balloon. But as yet no one had made a free flight.

Blanchard resolved to do so. He announced that he would make an ascent from the yard of the Walnut Street Prison in Philadelphia. Why a prison yard? The answer here, as it is to so many things in life, is money. In order to sell tickets, Blanchard needed an enclosed area protected by walls, where he could keep the paying customers in and the rest of the world out.

On Wednesday, January 9, 1793, a large audience, including President George Washington and the French ambassador, assembled in the prison yard to watch the great event. Unfortunately for Blanchard's finances, an even larger crowd of non-ticket-holders was outside the gates, watching from every street corner, window, and open field in the city.

A band played and the artillery fired salutes as the balloon was inflated with hydrogen. Just as Blanchard was ready to lift off, President Washington came forward to present him with a special letter, requesting citizens of the United States who encountered the Frenchman to provide him with "that humanity and good will, which may render honor to their country."

(Washington's letter, incidentally, seems to have vanished. Too bad: as the first airmail letter in American history, it would be worth a fortune to collectors.)

Blanchard took off a few minutes after 10:00 A.M. As he rose in the air he could see Philadelphia and the surrounding countryside spread below him and he could hear the shouts of wonder from the crowd. He waved a banner with the French tricolor on one side and the American stars and stripes on the other.

It was a fairly uneventful flight, easier certainly than his channel crossing eight years before. He performed experiments designed by Philadelphia scientists, like capturing air in bottles, testing magnets, and taking his pulse. The greatest problem came from a little black dog someone had given him to take along. The frightened animal got air sick and then spent the rest of the flight whining.

The wind took Blanchard to the southeast toward New Jersey. After about fifty minutes in the air, he brought the craft to a gentle landing in a clearing in the New Jersey woods. He had come down about fifteen miles from Philadelphia in what is now Deptford Township. A Jersey farmer was the first to find him. The startled Jerseyman was unable to read Washington's letter and could not understand Blanchard's French, but he did accept a swig of wine offered by the aeronaut. Some other locals arrived, and understood enough so that they were able to take Blanchard back to Philadelphia that evening.

Blanchard had triumphed, but disappointment followed. He was never able to raise enough money for another flight in America, and he finally returned to Europe, where he died years later in a balloon accident. But he was proud of having made the first aerial flight in the New World.

There has been one curious challenge to Blanchard's achievement. Some time in the distant past in a remote Peruvian plateau, miles of geometric lines were scratched into the ground by the native Indians. When seen from the air, and only from the air, these lines can be seen to form gigantic images of birds, spiders, and other objects. In the 1970s an amateur archeologist used this as evidence that the ancient Incas had mastered flight. To prove his point, he built a hot-air balloon using the type of fabric made by the Incas, and he took it up over the Peruvian plains. But as critics have pointed out, just because the Incas might theoretically have been able to construct balloons doesn't mean they did.

No, the credit for that historic first flight goes to Blanchard. And New Jersey gets a bit of the glory by just being there when he needed a place to land.

11 John Adams's Ass

The year 1798 was an important one for human creative expression. In London, Wordsworth wrote poetry; in Madrid, Goya painted frescos; in Vienna, Beethoven composed piano sonatas.

And in Newark, New Jersey, Luther Baldwin expressed the hope that the president of the United States would get hit by a cannonball in his rear end.

Baldwin was a gruff and grizzled captain of a Passaic River garbage scow, a fellow who enjoyed having a drink or two with the boys down at the local tavern. His rendezvous with history came one summer morning when President John Adams was passing through Newark on his way from the nation's capital in Philadelphia to his family home in Braintree, Massachusetts.

The leading citizens of Newark turned out with a band and an artillery company to salute the chief executive. As the president's coach made its way through the town, the artillery fired salutes, the church bells rang, and the president's supporters cheered.

What happened next was described by a local newspaper: "Luther Baldwin happening to be coming toward John Burnet's dramshop, a person that was there says to Luther, there goes the President, and they are a firing at his a——. Luther, a little merry, replies, that he did not care if they fired through his a——."

The type of low humor expressed by Baldwin is as old as human society. Shakespeare used the same kind of ribald jokes about the human anatomy to evoke laughter from his London audience. But where Shake-

John Adams, President of the United States of America
For daring to insult President Adams, a Newark tavern lounger ran afoul of the law. Library of Congress.

speare got away with it, Baldwin did not. He was arrested and charged with "speaking seditious words tending to defame the President and Government of the United States."

To understand why Baldwin was in such deep trouble for such an innocuous remark by today's standards, we have to go beyond the country town of Newark to weighty issues of national government and foreign affairs.

This was the age of the fearsome Napoleonic Wars between England and France. America was a new, weak country far from the European centers of power. But America was a proud country too, and the Federalist government of President John Adams bristled when the French government interfered with American shipping, hanged American seamen serving on

British ships, and demanded bribes from American diplomats in Paris. In retaliation, the American navy attacked French warships in the Atlantic.

The Republican Party of Thomas Jefferson (the forerunner of today's Democratic Party) admired the ideals of the French Revolution and felt kinship with France. Republicans bitterly attacked Federalists like President Adams, Alexander Hamilton, and even the sainted George Washington, for throwing America on the side of Great Britain.

Using their majority in Congress, the Federalists struck back at the Republicans by passing a series of laws aimed at suppressing dissent. These notorious Alien and Sedition Acts made it a crime to "threaten any officer of the United States Government with any damage to his character, person, or property" or to speak "in a scandalous or malicious way against the government of the United States, either House of Congress, or the President, with the purpose of bringing them into contempt."

Twenty-five people, including newspaper editors, journalists, and political leaders were arrested under the acts. Among them was Matthew Lyon, a fiery Republican congressman from Vermont, who became known as the "Spitting Lyon" for expectorating in the face of a Federalist opponent during a brawl in Congress. Another Republican convicted under the acts was the writer James Callender, who described President Adams as "a repulsive pedant, a gross hypocrite, and an unprincipled oppressor." By his intemperate remarks in Newark, Luther Baldwin joined this group of prominent lawbreakers.

Republican newspapers around the country such as the *Newark Centinel of Freedom*, the *Portsmouth Oracle of the Day*, the *Philadelphia Aurora*, and the *New York Argus* hailed Lyon, Callender, and others as martyrs. These feisty newspapers loved to skewer the pompous Federalists, and they gleefully spread the story of the lowly Newark tavern lounger and the mighty president of the United States.

The fact that the derriere of the president was involved made the story even better. One Republican newspaper observed, "Can the most enthusiastic federalists and tories suppose that those who are opposed to them would feel any justification in firing at such a disgusting a target as the ——— of J.A.?" Jokes were made about the fact that when the episode occurred, Adams was on the way to his family seat.

Republican newspapers described Baldwin as a good citizen, an honest man, and a friend to his country. Said the *Argus*, "When we heard that Luther Baldwin was indicted for sedition, we supposed that he had been guilty of something criminal . . . we must confess that our astonishment has been excessive on hearing the peculiarity of the expression for which so formal a trial was instituted."

The *Centinel of Freedom* opined that Baldwin had been arrested because the Federalist tyrants of Newark were "much disappointed that the president had not stopped that they might have had the honor of kissing his hand."

The chief informer against Baldwin was John Burnet, the owner of the tavern. Burnet was lambasted by Republican newspapers as a wretch who turned in his neighbor in order to win a job from the Federalists of Newark. The *Centinel of Freedom* asked of Burnet, "Of what materials must a man be composed, that he will become a voluntary informer against another for a mere expression, drawn from him when in liquor, that did not injure any one's person or property and by that means ruin a man and distress his family?"

Burnet evidently felt sorry for what he had done and is reported to have publicly declared that Luther was "a good citizen, an honest man, a friend to the country, and meant no harm in what he said."

To Republicans, the whole episode showed the incredible arrogance of the Federalists, and how they wished to cloak the president of the Republic with the same pomp and majesty as King George of England. The Federalists, warned the *Centinel*, wanted "to persecute and tread under foot all those who refuse to be duped into their measures."

Meanwhile, what of Luther Baldwin? The Federalists sorely wanted a conviction. Two heavyweight Federalists, Supreme Court Associate Justice Bushrod Washington and District Judge Robert Morris, presided over the trial. Faced with a hostile court, and with the fact that he did say what he was charged with, Baldwin pleaded guilty. He was fined $150 and costs of the trial.

History does not record how Baldwin came up with the money, or indeed what happened to him after his trial was over. But we do know that the abuses of the Alien and Sedition Acts helped to rally the nation behind the Republicans. In the election of 1800, the Republicans swept into control of the White House and Congress. It's not hard to imagine old Luther hoisting a glass in honor of the new president, Thomas Jefferson, in some Newark tavern.

The Alien and Sedition legislation expired, and along with them the Federalist Party. And today, as long as they do not threaten his life, Americans are free to make whatever tasteless remarks they feel like about the president's anatomy.

12 Man Eats Tomato and Lives!

The story of how Colonel Robert Gibbon Johnson ate a tomato on the steps of the Salem County Court House in September 1820 is one of the most dramatic and colorful in New Jersey history.

It seems that in the early years of the nineteenth century, Americans regarded tomatoes as "love apples," charming to look at but poisonous to eat. Colonel Johnson, a leading citizen of Salem County and a man with a passion for agricultural improvement, became convinced that the tomato was a healthy food that could enrich the local economy. He boldly announced that he would eat tomatoes from the steps of the Salem County Court House.

On the appointed day, hundreds of people gathered in the Court House square to watch as Johnson strode up the steps, carrying a bushel basket of tomatoes. He pulled one of the forbidden items out of the basket, and to the horrified gasps of the spectators, boldly bit into it. The crowd waited tensely for the colonel to fall to the ground in pain. But, amazingly, nothing happened.

Colonel Robert G. Johnson
There was a Colonel Robert Johnson, and he lived in Salem County, but there is no truth to the story that he was the first person to eat a tomato. Special Collections and University Archives, Rutgers University Libraries— New Jersey Portraits Collection.

From that day, the tomato took off in the United States, and soon became a staple of American cuisine. Thanks to the brave Colonel Johnson, our lives are enriched by pizza, spaghetti sauce, ketchup, Bloody Marys, and BLTs.

There is only one nagging problem with this magnificent tale of courage in the face of ignorance: it isn't true, from the stuff about the love apples to the business about Colonel Johnson.

The whole sordid affair has been exposed by a modern historian, Andrew F. Smith, who in 1990 published an article entitled "The Making of the Legend of Robert Gibbon Johnson and the Tomato," in the journal *New Jersey History*.

According to Smith, there was indeed a Colonel Johnson who lived in Salem County early in the nineteenth century. He was indeed a leading citizen, and he established the Salem County Agricultural Society. And indeed, Salem County did become a center of tomato growing in the United States.

But no diary, letter, newspaper, or other source from that era mentions any link whatsoever between Colonel Johnson and the tomato. Moreover, the tomato industry did not get started in New Jersey until almost half a century after the supposed event. It also turns out that tomatoes were well known and well eaten in the United States long before 1820. Colonial cookbooks, letters, and gardening manuals all mention the tomato. Thomas Jefferson, among other early Americans, regularly grew and consumed them. So the legend of Colonel Johnson eating tomatoes on the Court House steps is bunk.

Was there a nugget of truth underneath the legend? It might just have happened that although tomatoes were being eaten by big shots like Jefferson, folks in rural Salem County eyed them with suspicion. And it may be that Colonel Johnson had something to do with their introduction. But on the other hand, there are two other local accounts about the origin of the tomato in South Jersey that are at least equally probable. In one, the vegetable was introduced by some Philadelphia ladies visiting Salem County; in another, tomatoes were first grown by a Cumberland County farmer in 1812.

How did the Johnson legend get started? The first reference appears in a 1908 book on Salem County written by a local newspaper editor appropriately named William Chew. Chew stated flatly that in 1820 "Col. Robert G. Johnson brought the first tomatoes to Salem County in this year. At that time this vegetable was considered unfit for use by the masses." Note that Chew's account did not appear until almost ninety years after the supposed episode and note that it said nothing about the Court House steps.

The steps scenario made its first appearance in a 1940 book, *The Delaware*, by a nationally known author, Harry Emerson Wildes. According to Wildes, Colonel Johnson started agricultural societies and country fairs to push his enthusiasm for tomatoes. "Not, however, until 1820, when he dared to eat a prize tomato publicly on the Court House steps, would cautious South Jersey accept as edible the vegetable that is now its largest crop."

The legend took off from there. Colonel Johnson appeared during the 1940s in books on American history and travel. Each time the story became a little bit more grandiose, with more dramatic details. In 1949 a Salem writer, Joseph S. Sickler, pushed the tale as far is it could go. In Sickler's version, Colonel Johnson was not just the first person in Salem County to eat a tomato, he was the first one in the entire United States. Sickler added dialogue as well: he depicted Colonel Johnson mounting the steps of the Court House and shouting scornfully to the crowd, "I'll show you dumb blankety-blank fools these things are good to eat. What are you afraid of? Being poisoned? Well I'm not and I'll show you I'm not."

Historian Smith believes that Joseph S. Sickler was the person most responsible for the spread of the legend; it was he who told the story to Harry Emerson Wildes and other writers. Sickler was a newspaper reporter, state assemblyman, amateur historian, and Salem postmaster. Sickler lost his job as postmaster abruptly. He was never charged with any crime, but Smith says there was suspicion that he had misappropriated funds.

After Sickler left Salem, he went to New York City, where CBS hired him as a "historical consultant" for an episode in the radio series "You Are There," devoted to—you guessed it—the story of Colonel Johnson and the tomato. The show, which was broadcast nationally on Sunday, January 30, 1949, presented the story as historical fact. Listeners across America heard Colonel Johnson mounting the steps, heard the murmur of the crowd, and then heard the shouts of amazement when the tomato was consumed. The radio announcer piously told the listening audience that this was the first tomato consumed in the United States.

It was from this broadcast that the story truly entered the national consciousness. Having heard it once on the radio, Americans accepted it as fact.

Today you can find the story everywhere, perpetuated by college professors, newspaper reporters, and food experts. It appears as gospel, for example, in the book *Why We Eat What We Eat* by an editor of the *Wall Street Journal* who should know better.

So the tomato story has taken root in American history, every bit as firmly (and erroneously) as George Washington's cutting down the cherry tree and Humphrey Bogart saying "Play it again, Sam."

It would probably be a mistake to say that all of this is simply a case of falsehood. The saga of Colonel Johnson has about it the elements of classic myth, of the godlike hero publicly risking death in the service of his people. Prometheus ascended to heaven to bring back fire; Colonel Johnson ascended the Court House steps to bring back tomatoes. (Does it mean anything that tomatoes and fire are both red?)

Probably no one would have been more surprised to find that Robert Gibbon Johnson had become an American folk hero than the old colonel himself, who for all we know never touched a tomato in his life.

13 Explosion on the USS *Princeton*

On February 28, 1844, the president of the United States, the secretary of state, and other Washington heavyweights went for what they thought would be a pleasant cruise on a brand-new U.S. Navy warship. This junket turned out to be a spectacular disaster that shocked the nation and crippled the government.

At the center of the disaster was a Jerseyman, Captain Robert Stockton.

Stockton was part of a proud naval tradition in New Jersey dating from the early years of the republic. Among the hard-fighting sailors our state gave to the new nation were Commodore John Barry, hero of the Revolution; Captain Richard Somers, who died fighting the Barbary pirates; Commodore William Bainbridge, who commanded the USS *Constitution* in the War of 1812; and Captain James Lawrence, who gave the famous order "Don't give up the ship."

Stockton came from a notable Princeton family: his grandfather was a signer of the Declaration of Independence and his father was a U.S. senator. Stockton joined the navy at age sixteen, and during his career saw combat in the War of 1812 and later fought pirates and slave traders.

He was a larger-than-life figure: hot-blooded (he fought two duels), ambitious (he rose from midshipman to captain and became a player in national politics), vain (he once bought a ship and named it after himself), and wealthy (he inherited the family's mansion, "Morven," in Princeton).

He also had a keen scientific curiosity, which set him apart from most seamen—a traditionally hidebound lot. He was especially interested in the bold, new technology of steam, a power source that for the first time enabled humans to move over the open seas without being dependent on the fickle wind.

While visiting England in 1837, Stockton encountered a steam pioneer, the Swedish-born engineer John Ericsson. The Swede had built a steam tugboat driven by a screw propeller. The British navy had rejected the vessel, but Stockton was intrigued. He discussed with Ericsson the next step—building a screw-propelled warship.

Once back in the United States, Stockton successfully lobbied the government to produce such a ship. He was awarded the contract to build it, with Ericsson as the designer. To no one's surprise, Stockton was named the captain. It did not hurt that Stockton had friends in high places, including President John Tyler, of "Tippecanoe and Tyler too" fame.

Stockton named the ship the U.S.S. *Princeton,* after his home town. When it was christened with a bottle of American whiskey on September 5, 1843, the vessel was the most advanced warship in the world, as up to date for its time as a modern stealth fighter airplane. It had powerful high-pressure engines that could move the ship along at twelve knots per hour. Unlike other steamships of that era, with their paddlewheels and smokestacks, the Princeton's screw propeller and steam mechanism were housed invisibly below the water line. To the astonishment of spectators, the ship was able to knife effortlessly through the water without the normal billowing sails, churning paddles, or belching smokestacks.

The armament of the *Princeton* was also revolutionary. Two massive cannon, perhaps the largest ever manufactured, were mounted on the deck. Each gun was able to fire two hundred-pound cannonballs a distance of over three miles. These weapons were so unique that they were given nicknames: one cannon was the "Oregon" and the other the "Peacemaker."

Ericsson designed and built the Oregon. The much larger and heavier Peacemaker was built by Stockton himself when he decided that he wanted a second. As this suggests, the captain and the inventor had quarreled. They were both men of strong opinion, but Stockton was the one in command. Ericsson faded into the background.

After sea trials, Stockton's first port of call was New York, where the *Princeton* beat the passenger liner *Great Western* in a spectacular race. Then, after installing the mighty deck guns, he took the ship to Washington to show it off to the top brass.

Now we come to the fatal voyage of February 28, 1844. On board were three hundred distinguished guests, including President John Tyler, members of the cabinet, congressmen, senators, generals, admirals, and foreign diplomats. Wives and children were invited too, and the widower president brought along his young fiancée, the twenty-two-year-old Julia Gardiner. Ericsson was not invited.

The *Princeton* left Alexandria around noon and sailed down the Potomac. After taking the air on the deck and watching the firing of the Peacemaker, the guests repaired below deck for a strenuous lunch of duck, chicken, turkey, ham, beef, partridge, ice cream, and fruit, accompanied by many alcoholic toasts. The marine band played popular airs.

The ship was on the return journey in the late afternoon, when some of the junketeers thought it would be fun to see the Peacemaker fired once again.

Stockton was happy to oblige, and as guests crowded around on the deck, he pulled the lanyard to touch off the mighty weapon. Disaster ensued: the left side of the breech exploded with a roar and a cloud of smoke, sending shards of iron hurtling into the crowd of spectators. Two members of the president's cabinet died: Secretary of State Abel P. Upshur and Secretary of the Navy Thomas W. Gilmer. Also killed were Commodore Beverly Kenton, chief of the Navy Bureau of Construction; Virgil Maxcy, a diplomat; and Congressman David Gardiner, father of the president's fiancée. Two sailors from the gun crew and a servant of the president lay dead as well. Nine people were wounded. The screams of the survivors pierced the air and the blood of the dead and injured ran on the deck.

Stockton himself had been stunned by the explosion, but he pulled himself to his feet to take command of the chaotic scene. He took the ship back to Alexandria while surgeons cared for the wounded and crewman covered the dead with flags.

Luckily, most of the guests had remained below, including President Tyler and his fiancée. When she learned of her father's death, she fell into a faint.

The disaster caused national mourning; a state funeral was held in the Capitol, followed by a political scramble to replace the vacant cabinet positions.

A naval Court of Inquiry absolved Stockton of any blame. He had built the Peacemaker according to the latest scientific standards, the court found, and it had been fired with normal procedures. The court even commended Stockton for his quick response after the explosion.

Stockton went on to earn a distinguished record in the Mexican War. He captured Los Angeles from the Mexicans and became the military governor of the territory of California; the city of Stockton, California, was named in his honor. He returned to New Jersey, where he became U.S. senator and president of his family's Delaware and Raritan Canal company.

Ericsson, the technical genius, earned fame years later as the builder of the Civil War ironclad U.S.S. *Monitor*, regarded as the prototype of the modern warship.

As for the *Princeton*, the disaster gave the ship a bad reputation, and it was decommissioned and broken up for scrap five years later. Perhaps it should have been preserved as a monument to Murphy's Law.

14

Two New Jersey Soldiers in Confederate Prisons

"War is hell," said William Tecumseh Sherman, the hard-bitten Civil War general. He might have been thinking of the over two hundred thousand Union soldiers who suffered in Confederate captivity. Here is the story of two such POWs who hailed from New Jersey.

Captain Henry Sawyer at Libby Prison

On July 6, 1863, Captain Henry Sawyer of the Army of the Potomac sat down to write a letter to his wife, Harriet, back in New Jersey. "My Dear Wife," he began, "I am under the necessity of informing you that my prospect looks dark." He wasn't kidding.

Sawyer was a carpenter in Cape May when Fort Sumter was fired upon in April 1861. He was one of the first New Jerseyans to volunteer to defend the Union, and within a year and a half he rose from a private in the infantry to captain in Company K of the First New Jersey Cavalry. In June 1863, Captain Sawyer was charging the enemy at the Battle of Brandy Station, in Virginia, when he was struck by Confederate bullets. One passed through his thigh; the other went through his cheek and out the back of his neck; a third killed the horse he was riding and sent Sawyer crashing to the ground.

The wounded Sawyer was picked off the battlefield by the Confederates and after being patched up by their doctors was sent to Libby Prison in Richmond. The infamous Libby was a tobacco warehouse that had been converted to an overcrowded, drafty, filthy prison for Yankee officers.

A short time before Sawyer's capture, a brutal incident had occurred in the border state of Kentucky. Two Confederate captains were captured behind Yankee lines and accused of spying and recruiting for the enemy. A Union general, Ambrose E. Burnside, treated the two men as guerrillas. After a military trial, and despite Confederate pleas for mercy, he had them shot by a firing squad.

The South was outraged by Burnside's act and decided to seek revenge. The commandant of Libby Prison brought all the Yankee captains under his charge, including the newly arrived Sawyer, into a room for a grim lottery. The name of each captain was written on a slip of paper and placed in a box, and a Union chaplain was asked to draw the names of two officers who would be executed in retaliation. Sawyer was the first to be selected; the second was Captain John M. Flinn, of the Fifty-first Indiana Infantry.

Captain Henry Sawyer
Captured in the Battle of Brandy Station, Sawyer was taken to Libby Prison in Richmond, where he was threatened with hanging, in reprisal for the execution of Confederate prisoners in Union hands. From the Collections of the Newark Public Library.

Sawyer was allowed to write to his wife. Samuel Johnson once said, "Depend upon it, Sir, when a man is to be hanged in a fortnight, it concentrates his mind wonderfully." And Captain Sawyer's mind seems to have been wonderfully concentrated indeed. He carefully explained that he was to be executed. "My situation is hard to be borne, and I cannot think of dying without seeing you and the children." He directed her to collect his army pay and a $50 debt owed to him. "Oh," he wrote, "it is hard to leave you thus." His guards saw him sob as he finished the letter.

Sawyer and Flinn were sent to await death in a basement cell so damp that the clothes they were wearing began to mildew.

Now it was the North's turn to feel outrage. Sawyer's pathetic letter to his wife was published in the *New York Times*. At Mrs. Sawyer's urging, prominent New Jerseyans sought help from President Lincoln. The governor of Indiana, O. P. Morton, and other prominent Hoosiers agitated on behalf of Flinn.

According to one account, Mrs. Sawyer met with Lincoln to plead for her husband. It is not clear whether that meeting ever took place, but we do know that Lincoln took a personal interest in the case. It was he who ordered the commanding general of the Union Army, Henry W. Halleck, to seize the one man who could force the South to back down—General Fitzhugh Lee, the son of none other than the Confederate military leader General Robert E. Lee.

Fitzhugh Lee had been captured at the Battle of Brandy Station (the same battle in which Sawyer fought), and he was now being held at a Union fort in Virginia. Another captured Confederate officer, Captain Robert H. Tyler of the Eighth Virginia Infantry, was selected along with Lee. Lincoln directed the Confederate government to be informed that if Sawyer and Flinn were executed, Lee and Tyler would be hanged in reprisal.

Sawyer and Flinn, meanwhile, were becoming desperate. They wrote a letter to the Confederate authorities, begging not to be executed. They suggested that Union prisoners from General Burnside's command should be chosen instead, and actually named two Federal officers who were being held prisoner in Atlanta. Those who would condemn this letter as cowardly might want to imagine what it must have been like waiting for the executioner. At any rate, nothing came of this letter, except for contempt from Southerners who knew of it.

Sawyer had been told by the Confederates that his wife would be able to visit him in Richmond before he died. But when she approached the Confederate capital on a Union ship under a flag of truce, the Confederates forced her to return without seeing her husband. "When the Yankees conduct themselves like Christians in this intercourse with us, they may expect a like return," the *Richmond Examiner* said.

Even though Lincoln had declared that Fitzhugh Lee would be hanged the moment Sawyer and Flinn were executed, Southern opinion still demanded revenge. "The people call for death of these two Yankees, and it is useless to delay their deaths any longer," the *Examiner* said. At the same time, Northerners used the image of Sawyer and Flinn waiting for death in their grim dungeon as yet one more Confederate atrocity.

But under threat of reprisal, the South's desire for revenge gradually cooled. The two Union captains were removed from their basement confinement and permitted to be with the other prisoners in Libby. In return, the watch over Lee and Tyler was relaxed.

Finally, eight months after their names were drawn in the prison lottery, Sawyer and Flinn were exchanged for Lee and Tyler. The exchange took place between Union and Confederate lines at City Point, Virginia. Lee and Sawyer congratulated each other on escaping the hangman. It was a strange war.

Sawyer returned a hero to New Jersey. At a ceremony in Trenton, Governor Joel Parker commissioned Sawyer as a major in the cavalry. From there Sawyer went to Cape May, where he spent five months with his wife. There has probably never been as happy a vacation in Cape May before or since. Sawyer then rejoined his regiment and spent the last year of the war in General Grant's bloody, grinding death grip on the Confederacy.

After the war, Sawyer returned to Cape May. In 1876 he built the elegant Chalfonte Hotel and became its proprietor. Sawyer prospered; he was a respected member of the Cape May City Council and served a stint as superintendent of the New Jersey branch of the United States Life

Saving Service, making sure that rescue was ready for ships that foundered off the coast.

His hotel became a favorite destination for Southern families on vacation, and they were welcomed by Sawyer. The hotel still stands in Cape May, and Southern cooking is still a specialty.

It is pleasant to imagine Henry and his beloved Harriet rocking on the wide front porch of the Chalfonte, enjoying a Cape May twilight together. Perhaps they are holding hands. Perhaps they are thinking to themselves that sometimes in life there are happy endings.

Corporal Charles Hopkins at Andersonville

Ever since the Civil War, a debate has raged about Andersonville, the notorious prisoner-of-war camp in Georgia. Northerners argue that the place was deliberately brutal. Southerners reply that the Confederacy, disrupted by war and cut off from medicine by the Union blockade, could not provide for the prisoners.

For Charles Hopkins of Boonton, New Jersey, there was never much doubt about which side was right in that debate. He was convinced through his long life (he died in 1934 in his ninety-second year) that the Confederates sought to murder their Yankee prisoners through starvation, disease, and mistreatment. Old man Hopkins had a right to his opinion: he was a survivor of Andersonville.

At the Battle of the Wilderness in May 1864, the twenty-one-year-old corporal in the First New Jersey Infantry Regiment was captured by the enemy. Along with other prisoners, he was shipped south in a boxcar. On the way, he saw Confederates hang a black Union soldier.

The train stopped in Andersonville, and Hopkins was marched through the stockade gate. "Such a sight I have never seen," he wrote in his diary. The prison consisted of twenty-six acres surrounded by a high wooden fence. The captured Yankees were crowded together—as many as thirty-three thousand occupied the prison at one time. Dressed in shreds of uniforms, the captives had no shelter from the sun, rain, heat, and cold except for holes in the ground and makeshift tents. Guards shot prisoners who crossed the "dead line," seventeen feet from the stockade fence.

Corporal Charles Hopkins
A Boonton native who enlisted in the Union Army, Hopkins never forgave
the South for the horror he endured at the Confederate prison camp at
Andersonville, Georgia. From the Collections of the Newark Public Library.

To Hopkins, the worst part was the utter lack of sanitation. Water came from a meandering stream, which was used for latrines and for drinking water, forming what Hopkins described as "a mud of liquid filth." A stench hung over the prison. Lice, maggots, and flies were everywhere. The smallest sore became infected, and Hopkins reported seeing men dying of gangrene, with maggots infesting their bodies. What little food was given the prisoners was mostly vile; Hopkins recalled beans crawling with cockroaches and weevils.

In such a world, some men turned on their fellows. New prisoners thrown into the pen were called "fresh fish," and were robbed of their possessions by gangs of other prisoners known as "raiders." Hopkins and his New Jersey friends banded together to protect themselves. In July 1864, Hopkins watched in satisfaction as six of the raiders were hung, after a trial in which Union prisoners served as judge, jurors, and defense and prosecution attorneys.

In the midst of this disappointment, filth, and brutality, some men gave up and died. But Hopkins was motivated by his faith in the Union cause and his hatred of his captors. "Inhuman devils, the Confederates are, and no one can change the fact," he wrote in his diary. He was proud that most of his fellow prisoners supported the administration of President Lincoln even though they knew that back home, Democrats campaigned for an end to the war.

Hopkins's diary helped to sustain him. In it he recorded details of the weather, the mistreatment of the captives, and the hopeful rumors, which always turned out to be false, of how they would be exchanged for Confederate prisoners.

Why was there no exchange? Southerners say that it was the fault of Lincoln's government, which had overwhelming manpower and did not want to return captured Confederates to the enemy armies. Northerners say it was a matter of principle: there could be no exchange until the South agreed to include captured black soldiers.

Hopkins managed to escape three times. The first time, a fellow prisoner, who in civilian life had been a tailor, sewed him a Confederate uniform made from empty bean bags, and Hopkins nervously walked through the gate. Another time he escaped by tunneling underneath the stockade walls. Each time he was recaptured and returned to the prison. The prison commandant, Captain Henry Wirz, punished Hopkins by placing him in a stock that stretched him out in the Georgia sun. He bore the scars for the rest of his life.

In September 1864, after five months in Andersonville, Hopkins was transferred to another Confederate prison, this one in Florence, South Carolina. The new camp was less crowded and conditions were somewhat better. But by this time he was gravely ill from malnutrition and disease. His gums and teeth were rotting, and he described his body as skin and bone. He recalled later: "My limbs, from knees to toes, were swollen nearly to bursting, black purple in color, holes in which the finger could be inserted over an inch, putrid, disgusting to look at." The Confederate surgeons at Florence wanted to amputate his legs, but Hopkins convinced them to let him die with an unmutilated body.

Then came hope. As the war entered its last months, Union prisoners began to be paroled and sent North. Hopkins, who by now was unable to walk, crawled his way out of the prison hospital and dragged himself through ice and mud to the train, where he was finally transported to the Union lines. It was February 1865.

It took Hopkins two years to fully recover his health. As he recuperated back home in Boonton, he took satisfaction at the news that Captain Wirz died on the gallows—the only Confederate officer to be executed for war crimes.

Like Sawyer, Hopkins went on to live a productive life. He married and fathered seven children. He was awarded the Congressional Medal of Honor for an episode of bravery on the battlefield that occurred prior to his capture, and served as mayor of Boonton and member of the New Jersey Assembly. He was active in veterans' organizations and a loyal Republican.

He never forgave the Confederates. He visited Andersonville and took photographs of the places where he and his comrades had suffered. Around 1890, he wrote for his children a 280-page manuscript about his experiences as a prisoner of war, using his war diary as a source. It was a bitter document. It describes how the Confederates denied the prisoners pure water to drink or wood to build shelter or cook their food, despite the fact that the prison was surrounded by pine forests and abundant water.

While in the New Jersey Assembly, Hopkins supported a campaign to erect a memorial to the New Jersey soldiers imprisoned at Andersonville. The monument can be found today in the cemetery at Andersonville National Historic Site. It is a statue of a New Jersey soldier, facing south. On the base are these lines: "Go, strangers, to New Jersey; tell her that we lie here in fulfillment of her mandate and our pledge—to maintain the proud name of our state unsullied, and place it high on the scroll of honor among the states of this great nation."

Before you dismiss those words as Victorian sentimentality, think of what Charles Hopkins endured to preserve that great nation.

15 General Grant Skips the Theater

General Ulysses S. Grant loved his wife and he loved his children. He loved them so much that in order to spend some quality time with his family in New Jersey, he turned down an invitation from President Abraham Lincoln to attend a play at Ford's Theater.

In April 1865, Ulysses S. Grant was the Union's greatest hero. After years of failure for Northern armies, it was Grant who had brought victory. The news that Robert E. Lee had surrendered to Grant at Appomattox brought joy to the North.

Grant was the idol of the capital when he and his wife Julia arrived in Washington four days after the surrender. The couple were cheered by crowds everywhere they went; Julia recalled how joyous the city was, with cannons booming and flags waving and, at night, how public buildings were illuminated with candles in the windows. The next morning, April

14, Grant attended a meeting of the cabinet where he discussed the future of the country.

President Lincoln and his wife invited General and Mrs. Grant to go to the theater that night to see the comedy *Our American Cousin*. But after some hesitation, Grant declined. He politely informed the president that could not attend because he and Julia had arranged to travel by train to Burlington, New Jersey, to see their children.

Why Burlington? When Lincoln brought Grant to the East to command the Union armies in the spring of 1864, Mrs. Grant had looked for a place where she and the couple's four children could live. On the recommendation of a friend, she chose the quiet Jersey community of Burlington. The family's two daughters were enrolled in St. Mary's Hall, an Episcopal school for girls. (Many girls at the school had family ties to the South; once when Grant paid a visit some of the students sullenly refused to look at him.)

So instead of going to the theater, General and Mrs. Grant took the evening train from Washington headed north. The Lincolns found another couple, a young army major and his fiancée, to accompany them to the theater. And it was there while watching the performance, that Lincoln was slain by the demented actor John Wilkes Booth.

At 10:15 P.M., the moment the assassin's bullet ploughed through Lincoln's brain, Grant and his wife were speeding through the night, headed for Philadelphia. There is a belief that someone on the train, perhaps an accomplice of Booth's, tried to kill Grant. Julia felt she had been shadowed all day by a sinister-looking man who followed them to the train station. At one point on the train trip, someone tried to force his way into the Grants' locked car. The train crew stopped him, and the man got away. Years later, the Grants received an anonymous letter from a man who claimed that he had gone on the train that night to kill the general. The would-be assassin wrote that he was glad he had failed in his mission.

It was late at night when the Grants reached Philadelphia, still in ignorance of the assassination. In order to get to Burlington from Philadelphia in those days, it was necessary to take a ferry to Camden and then another train to Burlington. On the way by carriage to the Philadelphia ferry slip the Grants stopped at Bloodgood's Hotel, where Grant, who had not eaten since early that morning, had wired ahead for dinner.

But before he could eat his plate of oysters, he was handed a telegram. What must he have thought when he read the first sentence? "THE PRESIDENT WAS ASSASINATED TONIGHT AT FORDS THEATER AT 10:30 TONIGHT AND CANNOT LIVE." Julia noticed that he seemed pale as he read it. "Is there anything the matter? You look startled," she said. She cried when she learned the news. When they reached Burlington the Grants stayed up all night talking to neighbors. Before the sun rose, the general took a special train back to Washington.

The trip of Ulysses and Julia Grant to New Jersey that night leads to thoughts of "what if." What if the Grants had decided to postpone their trip to Burlington and instead went to the theater? Would history have changed? Grant was a celebrity to Washingtonians; more so than the familiar Lincoln who had lived there for four years. It might have been that with Grant present, the presidential box would have been more closely guarded that night, and perhaps the audience might have paid more attention to what was going on there. Maybe Grant himself might have seen the approaching assassin and stopped him from committing his terrible crime. Or maybe Booth might have slain both Lincoln and Grant, depriving the nation of a president and a future president.

In the 1930s Otto Eisenschiml, a chemist turned historian, thought it highly curious that Grant, a soldier trained to obey, would have turned down an invitation from his commander in chief. Eisenschiml concluded that only one man could have forced Grant to do so: Secretary of War Stanton, and that Stanton could have had only one motive—to get Grant out of the way so that the assassination of Lincoln could proceed unhindered. This led Eisenschiml to posit that Stanton was the moving force behind the assassination. Why? Because the radical Republican Stanton wanted the conciliatory Lincoln out of the way.

Eisenschiml's 1937 book, *Why Was Lincoln Murdered*, became a best seller, and spawned generations of books and documentaries that preach the same ludicrous theory about Stanton as the mastermind behind the plot to kill Lincoln. The book is a sort of granddaddy of conspiratorial books, like those showing that Lee Harvey Oswald didn't kill President John F. Kennedy.

But the real reason that Grant turned down Lincoln is a lot more prosaic. It has to do with the fact that Julia Dent Grant could not abide Mary Todd Lincoln one little bit.

It seems that Mrs. Grant had had several unpleasant experiences with Mrs. Lincoln. On one occasion, Julia Grant had hosted Mary Lincoln when the president came to inspect the army. To Mrs. Grant's humiliation, Mrs. Lincoln behaved in an erratic manner; at one point, she screamed hysterically when an officer's attractive young wife seemed to be flirting with the president. On a later visit to the front, Mrs. Grant fumed when Mrs. Lincoln neglected to invite her on board the presidential steamship.

So when Julia Grant learned that she and her husband had been invited to accompany the Lincolns to the theater that night, she sent a note to Ulysses informing him that he ought to decline the invitation, that she wanted to go back to Burlington to be with the children.

As it happened, Secretary of War Stanton also urged Grant not to attend the theater, on the grounds of safety. He had urged the same thing on Lincoln, but the president seemed determined to go. So probably it was some combination of Stanton's warning, Julia Grant's dislike for Mrs. Lincoln, and his own desire to see his children that prompted Grant to decline the president's invitation.

It is of such little domestic matters that great history is made.

16 The Jersey General and the Secret of Custer's Last Stand

You probably don't think of New Jersey as part of the Wild West. But in fact our little East Coast state is where two of the great symbols of the American West originated—the Stetson ten-gallon

General Edward Settle Godfrey in Full-Dress Uniform
A survivor of Custer's Last Stand, Godfrey kept a secret about the battle
for half a century. U.S. Army Military History Institute.

hat and the Colt revolver. The first Western movie, *The Great Train Robbery*, was filmed here in 1903. The man who discovered gold in California
and the man who discovered Pikes Peak in Colorado were natives of New
Jersey. Annie Oakley, star of Buffalo Bill's Wild West show, lived much of
her life in the Garden State (see chapter 23).

Another New Jersey link to the West is an old farmhouse in the rural village of Cookstown in New Hanover Township, Burlington County. The area was settled by English Quakers in the 1600s; the farmhouse itself was constructed around 1750 and was expanded and remodeled over the years, up to the 1930s. The building is now on the National Register of Historic Places and has been restored with the aim of making it a community center and museum, while preserving its original architectural character.

What qualified this house to be listed on the National Register was not its eighteenth-century origin, but rather the fact that it was the home of General Edward Settle Godfrey, who lived there for the last quarter century of his life, from retirement from the army in 1907 to his death in 1932.

Godfrey was a battle-hardened officer of the famed Seventh Cavalry in the Indian-fighting army of the nineteenth-century American frontier. He galloped the Great Plains on horseback, armed with carbine and pistol, his long mustache streaming in the wind. He was awarded the Congressional Medal of Honor for heroism and survived countless minor skirmishes and major battles of that era, including the famous Battle of the Little Bighorn, a.k.a. Custer's Last Stand.

A survivor of the Little Bighorn, you ask? Weren't Custer and the Seventh Cavalry entirely wiped out during that battle? Not exactly. Just before the battle, Custer divided the regiment into three separate battalions that maneuvered on different portions of the battlefield. It was the battalion Custer led that was killed to the last man. Most of the troopers in the other battalions survived after retreating to an elevation now known as Reno Hill, because it was held by Custer's second in command, Major Marcus A. Reno.

The Little Bighorn obsessed Godfrey for the rest of his life, and he carried into his retirement in New Jersey a secret about the battle—a secret he learned on the Jersey Shore. It is a story that has all the elements of a melodrama. Keeping a dark secret is a staple of literature. Shakespeare's plays, Verdi's operas, and Dickens's novels—not to mention just about every detective story ever written and every soap opera ever broadcast—hinge on the keeping of secrets.

The story begins at the battle of the Little Bighorn on June 25–26, 1876. Godfrey, a Civil War veteran and graduate of West Point, was then a thirty-two-year-old first lieutenant in Company K of the Seventh Cavalry. He performed with great heroism at the battle, at one point leading his company in a rearguard action against Indian attack. Faced by the onrushing Indians, Godfrey held his position by threatening to shoot any of his troopers who tried to run away. (Take a look at the man's determined face in those old photographs, and you get the sense that he was capable of delivering on that threat.) Historians of the battle believe that Godfrey's action saved Major Reno's position from being overwhelmed.

Two days after the battle, Godfrey was among the survivors from Reno Hill going to bury the dead on the field where Custer and his battalion met their doom. Riding next to Godfrey was another survivor, Captain Frederick W. Benteen. The two struck up a grim little conversation. According to Godfrey's later recollection of what was said, Benteen referred to something about Reno's conduct that, he told Godfrey, "would make your hair stand on end." Godfrey asked, "What is it? Tell me." At that moment another trooper riding by interrupted their conversation. "I can't tell you now," said Benteen. "Will you tell me some time?" asked Godfrey. "Yes," hissed Benteen. But sometime seemed never to come. Godfrey says that from time to time in the years that followed the battle he would raise the issue with Benteen, but Benteen remained silent.

Godfrey's life in the aftermath of the Little Bighorn was eventful. In 1877 he fought against the Nez Perce Indians at the Battle of Bear Paw Mountain in which he was seriously wounded, and for which he later was awarded the Medal of Honor. In 1879, along with other Seventh Cavalry officers, he testified before a military court of inquiry, called to look into the question of Major Reno's conduct at the Little Bighorn. Reno was acquitted of any wrongdoing, but it placed a stain on the man's career, and he was eventually discharged from the army. Also in 1879, Godfrey was appointed as instructor of cavalry tactics at West Point, where his lectures about Custer's Last Stand attracted wide attention.

It was in 1881, during his West Point years, that he went on a fishing trip with some friends, including Benteen, to the village of Point Pleasant on the Jersey Shore. The Jersey coast was a nationally known summer resort in those years. Presidents regularly visited the shore, including Ulysses S. Grant, who had a cottage in Long Branch, about twenty miles north of Point Pleasant. Point Pleasant was less posh than Long Branch and more isolated—it had not yet been reached by railroad.

Godfrey says that it was the evening, everyone else had gone to the beach for a swim, and he was alone with Benteen. Presumably Godfrey and Benteen were in a hotel or rooming house they had rented near the ocean. Here is how Godfrey later remembered the conversation:

> Godfrey: "Benteen, now we are absolutely alone, and no one can hear. You promised to tell me what you had in mind, and I want you to tell me now."
>
> Benteen: (after some hesitation) "Don't you think it is just as well to let bygones be bygones?"
>
> Godfrey: "No, I insist on your promise."
>
> Benteen: (after silence) "Well, on the night of the 25th Reno came to me after all firing had ceased and proposed that we mount every man who could ride, destroy such property as could not be carried, abandon our position, and make a forced march back to our supply camp. I asked him what he proposed to do with the wounded, and he replied 'Oh, we'll have to abandon those that can not ride.' I said, 'I won't do it.'"

So there it was. Godfrey now knew the sordid story—while besieged on the hill, Reno had contemplated leaving the wounded soldiers to a certain and painful death. In that frontier army, it was an utterly dishonorable and despicable thing to do.

That was the secret that Godfrey learned from Benteen, and a secret he kept from public sight for nearly half a century. But why did Godfrey keep mum? Out of respect for Reno? Unlikely. He had no particular regard for the man. It is more likely that Godfrey kept quiet out of a desire not to disgrace the Seventh Cavalry and its officers. Closing ranks to prevent outsiders from seeing the insiders' dirty linen is a common human characteristic in organizations and certainly characterized many of the survivors of the battle.

Life went on for Godfrey after the Point Pleasant revelation. There was some sadness and disappointment. His wife died in 1883, and he left

West Point to return to active service on the plains. He fought at the Battle of Wounded Knee in 1890, and his controversial role in that unhappy battle put a cloud over his reputation. The following year he was injured in a train accident. But there were accomplishments as well. Godfrey continued to be given other assignments in the army. He served in Cuba and the Philippines, taught at cavalry school, got promotions. For the purposes of this story, one important event during this time was his remarriage. His second wife was Ida Emley of Cookstown, New Jersey.

Through all of this, Godfrey never lost his abiding interest in the Little Bighorn, and he set about to write an article about the battle, using his West Point lecture notes as a basis and contacting old friends from the Seventh Cavalry to get their perspectives on that fatal event. His article, entitled "Custer's Last Battle," was published in the January 1892 issue of *The Century*, a popular American magazine. This article has been acclaimed as the first real analysis of the battle by a serious author. Historian Robert Utley describes it as "fundamental to any study of the Little Bighorn" and "a beacon of clarity and authority." In this pioneering article, Godfrey laid out the controversies that have preoccupied military historians and Custer buffs ever since. It was also remarkably well written. Godfrey provided powerful glimpses of what it must have been like to have been there, with the bullets fired by Indians making a terrifying "swish-thud" sound as they struck the ground, about the maddening thirst of the besieged men on Reno Hill, and about how, after the battle, the naked bodies of Custer's dead troopers seen from a distance looked like white boulders scattered over the field.

In the course of his research for the article, Godfrey received a letter from Benteen, who was panicked that Godfrey would reveal the secret of Reno's cowardice. Benteen called on his old friend to be charitable: "Don't you think that Reno has been sufficiently damned before the country that it can well be afforded to leave out in the article the proposition from him to saddle up and leave the field of the Little Bighorn on the 1st night of the fight?" Benteen need not have worried. In his *Century* article, Godfrey said only the following regarding the episode on Reno Hill: "The question of moving was discussed, but the conditions coupled to the proposition caused it to be indignantly rejected." No names, no indication of who did the proposing and who did the rejecting.

After serving for forty-four years in the army, Godfrey retired in 1907 with the rank of brigadier general. He moved with his wife to her family home in Cookstown, where he lived for another quarter century. He appears to have had a satisfying retirement—lucky man! He was an enthusiastic gardener and an active participant in veteran and fraternal organizations. He thoroughly enjoyed the visits from his grandson, Edward Settle Godfrey III. Retirement also gave him the leisure to indulge his fascination with the years of the Indian Wars in general and the Little Bighorn in particular. From his study at Cookstown he produced more articles for newspapers and magazines and kept up a steady stream of correspondence about the battle.

Godfrey was the guest of honor at the New York City premier of a silent movie depicting the Custer fight. To the audience at the theater he must have seemed like a living artifact from a time rapidly becoming as remote as ancient Egypt. A highlight of his life was his prominent role at the fiftieth-anniversary ceremony at the Custer battlefield in 1926. He attended the event with his grandson and, as a celebrity, was photographed with aged Indian survivors of the battle.

In these retirement years he became increasingly friendly with another survivor from the Little Bighorn era, Elizabeth Bacon Custer, the widow of Godfrey's slain commander. (Here's another New Jersey connection—after the Battle of Little Bighorn the widow moved East and spent a few months living in Newark, New Jersey, before moving to New York City.) Libbie Custer made a career of fiercely defending her late husband's memory from the slightest suggestion that he had made errors of judgment at the battle.

Godfrey was won over by the widow and, like her, grew ever more censorious of Reno. He campaigned along with her to keep any reference to Reno off a proposed historical marker at the battlefield. In his publications he described the manifold failures of Reno at the battle—Reno's hasty retreat to the hills and his failure to come to the support of Custer. But while he referred to Reno's proposal to abandon the wounded in his private correspondence, he kept carefully silent about it in his published writings.

And then, near the end of his life, he revealed his secret. He did so in dramatic fashion at the January 25, 1930, dinner of the Order of Indian Wars in Washington, DC. At that event he gave forth a torrent of words about the revelation from Benteen on the beach at Point Pleasant. Godfrey's remarks motivated another old veteran at the dinner to affirm that he had heard the same story about Reno from Benteen.

Why did Godfrey finally go public with a secret he had guarded for nearly a half century, from 1881 to 1930? In part because the story was beginning to surface in print. Four years before the dinner, he had recounted it in confidence to a newspaper reporter, H. L. Sloanmaker, who turned around and published it in the *Boston Post*. One has to fault Godfrey on this—it seems to be a good rule that if you want to keep a secret, you should not tell it to a reporter.

So that's one reason. A second, and one likes to think more important one, was that Godfrey, besides being a fine solider, was a fine historian, as his *Century* article indicates. As a historian, he felt an obligation to tell what he felt was the truth about the past. By this time almost all the principals at the Little Bighorn had passed on—Benteen had been dead for thirty-two years, Reno for forty-one. Godfrey knew that his own end was in sight and must have wanted to set the record straight before he, too, was silenced by the grave.

Was the story Godfrey finally revealed actually true? Some students of the battle think it was a malicious rumor created by Benteen to discredit his old enemy Reno. But if Benteen created the rumor, why did he insist so stoutly and continuously that it be kept secret? The likelihood is that the story about Reno that Benteen told Godfrey was correct.

On April 1, 1932, two years after the dinner, and fifty-six years after the Little Bighorn, Godfrey passed away. He was eighty-eight years old. Just before he died, he lapsed into a delirium, and from the words that escaped his lips it was evident that in his mind he was back on the Great

Plains as a dashing young officer in the Seventh Cavalry. Not a bad way to die.

Now let us jump ahead a half century after Godfrey's death. In the mid-1990s, workmen restoring his Cookstown house found a strip of metal, held in place in the attic rafters by a nail, about six feet off the floor. The object was identified as a nineteenth-century U.S. Army bayonet. During the quarter century he lived there, the general evidently used an attic room as his study, and as a military man, it is likely that he was the one who hid the bayonet in the nearby rafters. But why would he carefully place this weapon of war there? There is lots of room for speculation. Maybe he didn't know where to put it, and absent-mindedly stuck it there, only to forget all about it. Perhaps he was playing a scavenger-hunt game with his grandson when they got called down to lunch, and it just stayed there. But these scenarios are unlikely, given the fact that it was held in place with a nail. So maybe he hid it there because his wife didn't like weapons around the house, but that's mighty unlikely for a woman who married a hard-bitten cavalryman. She must have known what she was getting herself into when she wed him.

I like to think Godfrey hid the bayonet for the same reason people bury time capsules, keep diaries, or build pyramids—to keep something of themselves behind for future generations to come across and ponder. The bayonet may have had special meaning for Godfrey. The PBS television program *History Detectives* did a segment on the mystery of the hidden bayonet and concluded that Godfrey might have acquired it when he was a sixteen-year-old volunteer in the Union army and kept it with him as a memento of his military career.

When he looked at the bayonet in his last years, perhaps he was struck by a line from a poem by Robert Louis Stevenson (a friend of Libbie Custer's, by the way): "Steel true and blade straight." The same words were inscribed on the tombstone of Sir Arthur Conan Doyle, who died less than two years before Godfrey. It may be a farfetched idea, but perhaps in that bayonet in the rafters, the old cavalryman saw a symbol of his own lifelong fidelity to honor and to truth.

17 Poor Mary Smith

These days in New Jersey, Roman Catholics and Protestants get along in cheerful harmony; there is probably less antagonism between them than between fans of the American League and fans of the National League.

But in the nineteenth century it was a different story. Back then old-line Protestants who had dominated the state since the colonial era saw their world threatened by the tens of thousands of Irish Catholic immigrants who were pouring into the state and vying for political power.

In the year 1868, all of this hatred between Catholics and Protestants centered on Mary Ann Smith, a poor, illiterate, fifteen-year-old Irish immigrant girl.

Mary Ann's mother had died a few years earlier, and Mary Ann had left her father's home in Newark to become a live-in servant with Protestant families in the city. One of her employers, a Methodist music teacher, persuaded her to attend the Market Street Methodist Church, and after a time declared that she had converted to Methodism. Protestants in Newark regarded this as a victory for their cause.

On March 24, 1868, Mary Ann left the household where she worked and lived to run some errands. She never returned. It was learned later that she was in the Convent of the Good Shepherd in Manhattan, where she had been committed by her father.

Mary Ann's Protestant friends were outraged. They claimed she had been lured her to the home of a relative on the pretense that one of her cousins was sick; Catholics had then spirited her away to the convent where she was being forced, through fasting and hard labor, to renounce her new faith. They described the convent as "a Roman Catholic nunnery, used to coerce converted Catholics back to Romanism."

Father George H. Doane, a thirty-seven-year-old Catholic priest in the Newark cathedral, sent a letter to the *Newark Advertiser* to defend what had happened to Mary Ann. He said that he knew the girl and had long been concerned about her welfare. On March 24 she had gone to visit her aunt, and Doane had gone there to see her. He had talked to her and found her "very headstrong and untruthful." He persuaded Mary Ann's father that the only way to reclaim the girl was to take her to the Sisters of the Good Shepherd, which he described as a charitable reform school for wayward girls, where Mary Ann would be well cared for. Doane rejected the charge that he had stolen the girl from her faith. "Really, if anybody has been trying to proselytize, it is they, and not we."

Doane was a well-known figure in Newark. He had been born into a prominent Protestant family—his father had been the Episcopal bishop of New Jersey—but George Doane turned away from the faith of his family to become a Catholic. He was an educated, articulate spokesman for the Church, able to battle the Protestants on their own level. To the Protestant community, Doane was a notorious example of the dangers posed by the Catholics.

To rescue Mary Ann, the Methodist Preachers' Meeting of Newark filed a petition in the Supreme Court of New York State, claiming that she was being held prisoner against her will and demanding her release. The hearing began on June 17 in New York Superior Court in Manhattan. A Protestant lawyer, Mr. Lord, represented the ministers; the convent was represented by the Catholic T. O'Connor. Reporters from New York and New Jersey papers covered the case.

The Protestants' aim was to show that Mary Ann was a virtuous young person who was sincere in her conversion but who had been abducted by the Catholics for daring to reject the Roman Church; the Catholics wanted to paint her as a wild, immoral child who had to be saved from herself.

The first person to testify was Mary Ann herself, brought in to the court by Father Doane and the sisters of the convent. Mary Ann confirmed that she was being held at the convent against her will. She said she was surrounded by girls of low morals. She denied that she was a wayward child, although she admitted that before she had become a Methodist she had been a "giddy girl."

The Methodist music teacher who had employed her as a servant in his home and who had helped introduce her to his church said, "I never saw a more modest, chaste, and circumspect young girl than she was in her deportment and conversation." The minister of the Market Street Methodist Church confirmed that Mary Ann was a "respectable and modest girl" who faithfully attended worship. Another Methodist who had employed Mary Ann said, "I never knew her to keep bad company or late hours."

Now it was the Catholics' turn to put forth their argument that Mary Ann was a girl of loose morals who had been rightfully sent to the convent. Father Doane took the stand to describe Mary Ann as a "disobedient, stubborn, and an uninstructed, very ignorant person" who was not capable of reasoning. "I think she is carried away by her inclinations," he said.

Mary Ann's father, James Smith, took the stand. He explained that although Mary Ann had lived outside the home as a servant ever since her mother had died, he had maintained fatherly concern for her well being. He said that on Father Doane's advice he brought the girl to the Sisters of the Good Shepherd. "I placed her there because she was misbehaving, keeping bad company, and late hours, and disobeying me. She is there now by my authority, and kept there by my will." The Protestant lawyer accused Smith of being a drunk; Smith retorted that he had only an occasional glass of beer and had not been drunk in some time.

Other witnesses said that Mary Ann stole from her employers and hung about with disreputable men at a notorious stable in Newark, implying that she was a prostitute. Two stable hands said they had had sex with the girl. In cross-examination it was brought out that both men had spent time in jail. Mary Ann returned to court to deny the charge of immorality.

After the testimony was over, the presiding judge observed that the case was a tangled one, but that Mary Ann was a minor and her father had the legal authority to commit her. The judge ruled in favor of the Catholics. Observers in the courtroom said that Mary Ann wept.

The Protestant-leaning press expressed outrage. *Harper's Weekly* stormed: "If a girl is being punished for preferring the Methodist to the Roman faith it is a matter of the profoundest public concern." The

Evening Journal of Jersey City declared that the episode was an example of "priestly deception and tyranny."

The Protestants hoped to appeal the decision, but then came a bombshell. Father Doane sent to the newspapers a letter he said had been sent to him by Mary Ann. "Be so kind, Rev. Father, as to put a stop to my trial as I consider there is but one true religion, and in that I mean to live and hope to die. I confess myself a Catholic now, and I hope forever." She expressed the desire to become a nun. Although some Protestants thought this was a forgery, there was nothing that could be done. The rumor arose a few years later that Mary Ann had left the Church and resumed life as a Protestant. But the story was unsubstantiated, and thereafter she seems to have disappeared from history.

Father Doane did not. He stayed in Newark and lived on into a more tolerant era. He became a respected figure in the city and worked to establish parks, hospitals, libraries, and public works. When he died at age of seventy-five, in 1905, he was mourned by Protestants and Catholics alike. No mention was made of the painful Mary Smith episode of thirty-seven years before.

Time really does heal wounds.

18 Mrs. Stanton Steps Out in Tenafly

In November 1880 an elderly lady shocked the citizenry of Tenafly, New Jersey, by attempting to perform a forbidden act in public. Had she been lewd? Drunk? No, Mrs. Elizabeth Cady Stanton, sixty-four, had tried to cast a ballot in an election.

Stanton was born in 1815 to a wealthy family in upstate New York. When she was eleven, her older brother died. The body was placed in a casket in the parlor, which was darkened and draped in mourning cloth.

Elizabeth Cady Stanton
A leader of the women's suffrage movement, the sixty-four-year-old Stanton shocked her Bergen County neighbors when she dared to cast a ballot in the 1880 presidential election. Special Collections and University Archives, Rutgers University Libraries.

When the young Elizabeth entered the room, she saw her father sitting sorrowfully next to the casket.

She climbed on her father's knee, and he put his arm around her. "We both sat in silence, he thinking of the wreck of all his hopes in the loss of a dear son, and I wondering what could be said or done to fill the void in his breast. At last he heaved a deep sigh and said: 'Oh, my daughter, I wish you were a boy!'" It was a memory that burned in her mind for the rest of her life. When she was a twenty-five-year-old newlywed, she and her husband journeyed to London to attend an international gathering of antislavery activists. Before the conference could get down to business, a debate flared about a motion to allow the admission of women attendees as delegates. The motion was soundly defeated, and Elizabeth Cady Stanton stormed out.

Once back home she began to talk to other women who, like her, were affronted by the way they were treated in the world of men, and she took the lead in organizing the first women's rights convention, held at Seneca Falls, New York, in 1848. As much as anybody, Stanton deserves to be considered the Founding Mother of the woman's suffrage movement.

Stanton did not live the life of a radical. She spent much of her adult life at home raising her seven children while her husband was away on business. But she had a deep vein of anger. "When I think of all the wrongs that have been heaped on womankind, I am ashamed that I am not forever in a condition of chronic wrath, stark mad, skin and bone, my eyes a fountain of tears, my lips overflowing with curses, and my hand against every man and brother."

She also had a strong ego and could be overbearing in pursuit of her cause. She argued that white, American women had more of a right to vote than immigrants off the boat and newly freed slaves. It was a position that helped to split the woman's rights movement.

Stanton probably needed her immense ego to survive the abuse she took. She was ridiculed not only for her campaign for the vote, but also for advocating a woman's right to hold a job, to divorce her husband, and to wear less restrictive clothing. (As a young woman, Stanton startled her neighbors by wearing a sort of pants suit called "bloomers.") She was criticized when she publicly defended a prostitute who was put on trial for the murder of an abusive john.

When her children were grown enough to give her some freedom, she became a regular speaker on the national lecture circuit, spending most of the year traveling around the country. To provide a refuge, she moved in 1868 from Manhattan to the little Bergen County town of Tenafly. She loved the pure air of New Jersey and the beautiful sunsets she could see from her suburban home. By this time she had distanced herself from her husband, who remained in the city.

As she approached old age, she decided the time had come to put down on paper what she knew about the struggle for equality. She invited her longtime friend and ally Susan B. Anthony to come to Tenafly to help her write what eventually became the classic two-volume *History of Woman Suffrage*.

The two old veterans of the struggle were strikingly different in appearance. Stanton was chubby with curly hair and a mischievous smile; Anthony was thin and severe and wore her hair in a tight bun. They complemented each other well. Stanton described her relationship with Anthony: "I forged the thunderbolts, she fired them."

In the midst of writing their history, they took time off for a bit of protest. It was a presidential election year, and on election day, November 2, 1880, a carriage was hired by the town Republicans to pick up GOP voters. When the carriage, bedecked with American flags, lumbered up to Stanton's house, she and Anthony climbed aboard. Stanton announced to the flabbergasted driver that since there were no men at home, she would do the voting.

When they arrived at the polling place, at a local hotel, the election officials tried to stop them. Stanton declaimed that she was entitled to vote on the grounds that she was a tax-paying, property-owing citizen of Tenafly, who was able to read and write and who was three times the legal voting age.

By this time a crowd had gathered. Some were favorable to Stanton and urged her on. But a state senator who was present demanded that she be excluded. He commanded the polling officials: "Put an end to this and go on with your voting. It has been delayed long enough for a small matter."

Stanton stood her ground. Drawing up her impressive bulk she announced, "Gentlemen, this is the most momentous question the citizens of your town have ever been called upon to decide." She and her friend Anthony cited passages from the United States and New Jersey constitutions to support women's right to vote. Stanton pointed out that in the early years of the century, women had been allowed to vote in New Jersey.

The poll inspectors were confused. Two tried to look the other way, but another wrapped his arms around the ballot box and covered the slot with his hand: "I know nothing about the constitutions, state or national."

He said, "I never read either, but I do know that in New Jersey, women have not voted in my day, and I cannot accept your ballot."

Stanton haughtily handed her ballot to the man, and told him severely that on him would rest the blame for denying her the fundamental rights of a citizen.

Back home, Stanton gleefully wrote a letter to two of her grown children about the episode:

> I had great fun frightening and muddling those old Dutch inspectors. The whole town is agape with my act. A friend says he never saw Tenafly in such excitement. The men have taken sides about equally. This is a good example of what I have often said of late that acts, not words, are what is needed to push this woman suffrage question to the fore.

It was a bold gesture, although it did not do much to hasten suffrage. Women did not get the right to vote in New Jersey until the passage of the Nineteenth Amendment four decades later. Mrs. Elizabeth Cady Stanton (she never let anyone call her Mrs. Henry B. Stanton) would have said it was about damn time.

19  It's About Time

Without looking at your watch, do you know what time it is? Chances are you can come pretty close to the correct time.

But wait a minute. What, after all, is "correct" time? For most of human history, time was determined by the position of the sun. When it was directly overhead, the time was noon.

The problem is that noon occurs at a different time depending on your position on the Earth's surface. For example, the sun is directly above Boston twelve minutes before it is above New York. Back in the early years of the country, it didn't bother anyone that high noon in Boston was 11:48 A.M. in New York. The two cities simply set their clocks differently, as did cities and towns around the nation.

So things might have long remained had it not been for a bright New Jersey lad, William Frederick Allen, who was born in Bordentown in 1846 and who as an adult lived with his wife and children in South Orange. Allen was a railroad man. At age sixteen he went to work for the Camden & Amboy Railroad and by his early twenties was the line's chief engineer. When he was twenty-six he took a new job as editor of the *Official Guide of the Railways and Steam Navigation Lines in the United States and Canada*, the nation's main compendium of railroad timetables.

Allen recognized that the patchwork system of local time was a nightmare for America's railroad lines, each of which set its clocks and its schedules according to the time of its headquarters city or of the main city in its region. A husband and wife travelling from, say, Boston, Massachusetts, to visit friends in Columbus, Ohio, faced a hodgepodge of conflicting timetables every time they changed from one line to another. Allen calculated that American railroads were operating on fifty different time schemes.

Allen made it his mission to end this confusion by establishing uniform time zones across the nation. He got himself appointed to the post of secretary of the General Time Convention, an organization of like-minded railroaders, and for a decade he lobbied astronomers, geographers, meteorologists, engineers, telegraph operators, railroad owners, and government officials to persuade them that America needed a standard clock.

There was not enormous public support for the idea. After all, most Americans in those years were farmers, and lived much as people always had, getting up when it was light and going to sleep when it was dark, planting and harvesting when the seasons changed. Even for a merchant or factory owner it made little difference whether time in one town matched the time in another.

So most Americans seemed perfectly happy with the local time they had grown up with. The U.S. Senate looked into the matter and rejected any reform on the grounds that trying to change time was as difficult as it would be to introduce new weights and measures. (The Senate had a point; look how the United States has avoided the worldwide metric system.)

Allen decided that the only way to accomplish the change was for the railroads to do it by themselves without waiting for the government or its citizens to agree. He drew up a map of the United States divided into four time zones—Eastern, Central, Mountain, and Pacific. Time was made uniform for all cities and towns within each zone, so that in the Eastern Time Zone, for example, noon was exactly the same moment in New York and Boston. Crossing from one zone to another, standard time changed by exactly one hour.

One of the cleverest parts of his scheme was the boundaries between the zones. They had little to do with state lines, mountains, or rivers. Instead, the boundaries were based on the junctures between major railroad lines.

For the technically minded, herewith is a technical explanation. Each of Allen's four time zones was roughly fifteen degrees of longitude wide. The time in each was based on a longitudinal line (or meridian) that ran down the middle. For example, noon in the Eastern Time Zone was defined as the time the sun was directly over the 75th meridian. Central Time was defined by the 90th meridian, Mountain Time by the 105th, and Pacific Time by the 120th.

Allen sent his proposal to every American railroad and got most of them to agree to the change. The time set for the transition to the new system was noon on Sunday, November 18, 1883, a date that became known as the "day of two noons."

All across the country on that day, trains stopped in their tracks at local noon while conductors reset their watches to the new time, and then started up again. Crowds gathered in cities to observe clocks get reset. In Trenton, the time was set ahead by one minute and three seconds, in Newark, clocks were set back by precisely three minutes, forty-eight and a half seconds.

In the crossroads state of New Jersey the change was welcomed. The *Trenton Times* editorialized that although the change was complex, it "will prove so advantageous and popular that no one will desire its abolishment." When a female customer in Newark's Lackawanna station asked for a new schedule, the proud clerk replied, "No, madam, we don't fix the timetable, we fix the clock."

But in some other parts of the country there was outrage that the old way of keeping time had been taken away by the powerful railroads. A letter writer to a Kentucky newspaper demanded to know "if anyone has the authority and right to change the city time without the consent of the people, and what benefit Louisville can derive from it." The newspaper agreed with the writer that the change was a Yankee attack on states' rights.

A leftist in Boston said that the change was a "piece of monopolistic work adverse to the workingman's interest." The voters of Bangor, Maine, voted overwhelmingly to hold on to their old time.

But most Americans became used to the new system, and it was finally adopted by the federal government in 1919. Today the nation's standard time remains much as Allen designed it in 1883. Allen became a nationally known figure. A New York reporter joked that he could be seen striding down Broadway with a precise step, as if on his own internal timetable.

In his book *Keeping Watch: A History of American Time*, the historian Michael O'Malley writes that Allen's invention of standard time was a milestone in the transformation of America from a collection of isolated, local communities to a modern, unified, industrial nation, dominated by big organizations like the railroads.

There's much truth to that. We can be nostalgic about an age when everything was local; when life was ordered by the bell in the village steeple. It was an age when there were no DVD players to program, no conference calls to make, and no jet planes to catch—a time when people weren't slaves to that little god we strap on our wrists every morning.

20 Leprosy in the Laundry

Anyone deluded enough to think that the good old days were better than our own era should spend some time leafing through the yellowed pages of antique newspapers (or more likely, reeling through microfilm versions of those papers). The press in the nineteenth century delighted in running stories of human misfortune, the more grotesque the better. These sordid accounts, which usually appeared on the front page, documented crime, accidents, suicide, illicit sex, domestic quarrels, and madness—all reported with some combination of moral outrage and sly humor. One might well ask why the papers gloried in that sort of thing. The answer is exquisitely simple—titillation sells newspapers.

This lurid style of reporting had been perfected during the 1830s in New York penny press newspapers like the *Sun* and the *Herald* and soon crossed the Hudson to New Jersey. Herewith is a sampler of one dozen assorted bizarre headlines from New Jersey newspapers during the height of the Victorian age. The stories behind each headline reveal something of the quality of life—or lack of same—in that long ago time.

"TIRED OF LIFE"
Sussex Independent, 1884

This newspaper article from rural west Jersey tells the story of the unfortunate Joseph Berry, age twenty-three. Distraught over the fact that his wife had left him, Berry journeyed to a secluded spot near the home of his wife's parents, where his spouse had presumably fled. There he swallowed poison, which caused him to cry out in agony. The commotion caused a physician to come to his aid. Said the account, "The Dr. administered the strongest emetics known to the profession, which caused the would-be suicide to vomit the vile poison in large quantifies," and Berry survived. Perhaps as helpful advice to others contemplating self-destruction, the newspaper observed, "Had his groanings been less audible he would possibly have been permitted to die undisturbed."

"SENTENCED FOR KILLING HER HUSBAND"
Plainfield Evening News, 1887

This story tells of Mrs. Catherine Keevan of Somerville, who dispatched her husband by "crushing his head with a sugar bowl." She was sentenced to nine years at hard labor for the crime. The newspaper observed that this might seem to be a short stretch in jail, but that given her age it amounted to a life sentence. Mrs. Keevan was sixty-eight.

"NOT FOXY BY NATURE"
Newark Journal, 1888

Political correctness was not a major concern for newspapers in this era, and this story uses vaudeville-style dialect to lampoon the Irish immigrant population. Mary Fox of Halsey Street in Newark is quoted as telling a courtroom judge, "I'm foxy be name but I'm not foxy be natur'. I always spake the truth an' I'll not deny that I was drunk last night." To which the judge cheerfully replies, "Candor is a good thing, Mary, but it will not help you this time. Ten days." While meant to be amusing, the story reveals the widespread alcoholism that lay behind many episodes of crime, violence, and misfortune. It was why so many reformers felt that Prohibition was the key to improving the human condition.

"AS HE WAS ABOUT TO ELOPE"
Newark Journal, 1888

Stories of runaway spouses were frequent in the era when it was easier to disappear than to get a divorce. In this instance a wife, Mrs. Katie Voigt, learned that her husband, John, a barber, was planning to depart for Cleveland, Ohio, with another woman. The wife, who had a child to care for, called the police. The lawmen collared her erring spouse, described by the paper as a "prince of the razor," just as he was preparing to leave his Mulberry Street barbershop in Newark to start his new life. He did, in fact, get to start a new life, but thanks to the local magistrate it was one behind bars.

"THE WILD MAN OF SUSSEX"
Newark Journal, 1888

Public displays of insanity were frequently reported on. This story concerns a deranged man who was apprehended in Sussex County where, the article reported, "he lived in the woods, ate only apples, peeped in the windows of houses, and frightened women and children." The story made the Newark newspapers when the Wild Man of Sussex went berserk while being escorted by the authorities through the city's Broad Street Station.

"KILLED AND EMBALMED BY ONE DOSE"

Newark Journal, 1888

Newspapers were filled with reports of accidents—people thrown to the ground by runaway carriage horses, struck by oncoming locomotives, mutilated by factory machinery. The accident in this story is unusual. It seems that one John Kennedy was attending the funeral of his niece in Garfield when he developed a thirst. Rummaging in a closet of the funeral parlor, young Kennedy found what he thought was a bottle of gin. But alas for him, it was not gin at all, but rather embalming fluid, the consumption of which brought about his premature demise.

"HIS FINGERS BITTEN OFF"

Evening Journal (Jersey City), 1890

A baker named Rangel and a barrel maker named Hinchey got into a nasty brawl in Jersey City. When taken up by the police, Hinchey stated that three fingers of his left hand had been bitten off by his opponent. Rangel professed that he had absolutely no idea how the other man came to lose his digits. The police let both men go. The story gives a whole new meaning to the term "finger food."

"AN ITALIAN ATTACKS HIS WIFE WITH AN AXE"

Evening Journal (Jersey City), 1890

Pasquale Pape of Hoboken, described by the paper as "fierce looking," attempted to kill his spouse with an axe. Fierce yes, but effective no—his wife, described as "not dangerously hurt" in the episode, informed the judge that her husband had tried unsuccessfully to kill her three times previously while she was sleeping.

"THREW HER MAN DOWNSTAIRS"

Evening Journal (Jersey City), 1890

For knocking her husband downstairs, a Jersey City woman, "big Ellen O'Connor" of Twelfth Street, was brought before a judge. In her defense, she said that her drunken husband had frequently thrown her down the stairs. Big Ellen added a poignant explanation for their constant quarreling: "The trouble is we have no children." In an era that saw large families as a source of comfort and economic security in old age, childlessness had chilled their marriage.

"LEPROSY IN LAUNDRY"
Paterson Evening News, 1897

If there was a Pulitzer Prize for irresponsible journalism, this newspaper article would be a strong contender. An unfortunate Chinese immigrant, Sam Lee, was found gravely ill at the Paterson laundry where he worked and was taken to the hospital. In purple prose, the reporter stated that some unnamed persons "assert the man has leprosy and people had better burn laundry clothes." The article spoke ominously of this "most dread plague of the Orient" and of "that disease which above all others the human family has dreaded." But at another point in the article, after discussing the opinion of the town's medical authorities, the reporter indicated that Lee's condition might have been tuberculosis, an enormously more likely diagnosis, given the absolute rarity of leprosy, and the widespread incidence of TB. But why let facts get in the way of a great headline?

"SUES FOR HEARTEASE"
Paterson Evening News, 1897

This story is a classic case of "he said/she said." The he was Mr. William H. Smith, a wealthy scion of a distinguished Paterson family. The she was Miss Anna Whelan, described in the article as "the pretty Hamilton Avenue nurse girl." Mr. Smith, who was a widower, had hired the young woman as a governess for his infant children. According to Miss Whelan, once she had moved into the household, Smith seduced her by promising marriage, but when she became pregnant he broke his promise and fired her. She struck back by suing him for $10,000 for breach of promise. The newspaper reported that at the trial, "Smith denied any love-making or promise of marriage. He had treated the girl as a servant and nothing more." The defense argued that the governess had gotten pregnant from one of her many male friends and had used her condition to extort money from her rich employer. Who was telling the truth and who lying? The members of the jury could not decide and the judge dismissed the case as a result of the hung jury.

"SHOCKING ACCIDENT"

Trenton Times, 1900

Let us close with this account of the unfortunate Thomas Allen of Trenton, who was answering the call of nature in the outhouse behind his home when he had the misfortune of falling through the floor. Allen "would have smothered in the pit below into which he sank up to his arm pits had he not had the presence of mind to grab on the joists and shout for help." An alert neighbor came to his rescue and hauled him out from his "perilous and undesirable" situation. One might observe that Allen had been, quite literally, in deep doo doo.

21 Stephen Crane Gets into Trouble

On August 17, 1892, the New Jersey chapters of the Junior Order of United American Mechanics, a workingman's organization, held their annual parade in Asbury Park. Among the spectators was Stephen Crane.

We remember Crane, who was born in Newark, as the author of a classic American novel, *The Red Badge of Courage*. But on that day in Asbury Park he was a skinny twenty-year-old kid, trying to break into the newspaper business.

That summer, as he had in the past, Stephen had come down to the Jersey Shore from New York to work as a cub reporter for a news service run by his older brother, Townley Crane, which supplied articles to the *New York Tribune* and other out-of-town papers. Under his brother's direction, young Crane wrote about piano recitals, church meetings, society doings, and boardwalk entertainment which appeared under headlines like "Joys of Seaside Life" and "Well Known People Who Are Registered at the Various Hotels." This was the sort of filler that big-city journalists lampooned as "The Flunkey-Smiths of Squedunk Are at the Gilded Pazaza Hotel for the Season."

A typical piece by Stephen ran: "A highly attractive feature of social entertainment at the Lake Avenue Hotel during the past week has been the informal piano recitals given by Miss Ella L. Flock of Hackettstown, N.J."

But there was something deeper in the young reporter: a rebellion against smug respectability. Perhaps in reaction to his quiet, safe religious upbringing, he deliberately lived the type of life his parents would have objected to and that strained his fragile health: drinking beer, playing poker, shooting pool, and smoking cigars. He was fascinated with the dark side of humanity, and when in New York he would disappear into the Bowery to observe the life of prostitutes, drunkards, petty thieves, and other flotsam of urban life.

Crane managed to keep his rebellious spirit out of his newspaper articles, except for an occasional jab, such as his description of a boardwalk attraction as "a gigantic upright wheel of wood and steel, which goes around carrying little cars filled with maniacs, up and down, over and over."

But then came the parade, and the renegade Stephen Crane burst forth. It was in late August, just at the end of the tourist season. Crane was coming out of a billiard parlor where he had gone for a cigar, when he witnessed hundreds of New Jersey members of the Junior Order of United American Mechanics marching down the street.

Something about that homely parade touched Stephen Crane, and when the last marcher passed by he went back to the office to dash off an article for the *Tribune*. The story he wrote was far different from the sort of pieces he had been writing that summer. He described the parade as probably "the most awkward, ungainly, uncut and uncarved procession that ever raised clouds of dust on sun-beaten streets." He spoke of the bent and dirty marchers in their shabby clothes, plodding along without quite understanding what their lives were all about.

But to Crane, these men at least had a certain dignity and honesty, in contrast to the rich, bored vacationers who watched the parade go by. The onlookers, he wrote, were dressed in "summer gowns, lace parasols, tennis trousers, straw hats, and indifferent smiles."

Crane took a slap at the local merchants as well: "The bona fide Asbury Parker is a man to whom a dollar, when held close to his eye, often shuts out any impression he may have had that other people possess rights. He is apt to consider that men and women, especially city men and women, were created to be mulcted by him."

"Asbury Park creates nothing," he wrote. "It does not make; it merely amuses. . . . This is a resort of wealth and leisure, of women and considerable wine."

Townley Crane would probably have prevented Stephen from sending such a bitter piece to the *Tribune*, but the older brother was away, most likely on a fishing trip, and didn't see it until too late. When the article arrived, the editor on duty at the *Tribune*'s office in New York probably would have trashed it too, but as he apologetically wrote later, he was just too busy handling the important news of the day to read it carefully. He placed Crane's piece in the Sunday edition under the innocent title "Parades and Amusements."

The story might still have gone unnoticed except for the fact that it was a presidential election year, and the owner of the *Tribune*, Whitelaw Reid, was the Republican nominee for vice president of the United States. Democrats leaped on the *Tribune* story, and gleefully distorted it to make it sound as if Reid's arch-Republican newspaper was attacking working-class Americans.

One indignant member of the Junior Order of United American Mechanics wrote a blistering letter to the *Tribune*, criticizing the "uncalled-for and un-American criticism" leveled at the patriotic organization of American-born citizens. An Asbury Park newspaper blasted the anonymous writer of the article who "thought it smart to sneer at the Juniors for their personal appearance and marching."

The embarrassed *Tribune* issued an editorial apology. "We regret deeply that a bit of random correspondence, passed inadvertently by the copy editor, should have put into our columns sentiments both foreign and repugnant to the Tribune. . . . It can scarcely be necessary to say that we regard the Junior Order of United American Mechanics with high respect and hold its principles worthy of all emulation." The apology didn't much help; Reid's Republican ticket lost the election.

Of course, everybody had missed the point of Crane's piece. He wasn't insulting the marchers so much as the rich who looked down on them.

Stephen and his brother Townley got the axe: articles from the news bureau were no longer welcome in the *Tribune*. But the younger Crane seemed to be pleased and surprised at the power of his words. "You'd hardly think a little innocent chap like me could have stirred up such a row in American politics," he boasted. "It shows what innocence can do if it has the opportunity."

When Crane returned to New York after the scandal, the *Tribune* editor who had mistakenly run his parade piece (and was called on the carpet for it) took Crane aside and suggested that a writer with his talent should stop wasting his time producing empty fluff.

Crane took that advice. He retrieved a manuscript he had been working on fitfully for years, rewrote it, and borrowed money to get it published. The book was *Maggie: A Girl of the Streets*, now considered a pioneering novel of social realism. It is suffused with the same anger as the article about the Junior Mechanics. It was followed by *The Red Badge of Courage*, along with short stories, poems, and frontline reports from the Spanish-American War. Between that summer in Asbury Park and his premature death from tuberculosis eight years later at age twenty-eight, Crane became one of the greatest writers in the English-speaking world.

The parade of the Junior Mechanics had quite unexpected consequences for Stephen Crane and for American literature.

22 The Ghostly Sphynx of Metedeconk

There is another piece of Stephen Crane's writing that deserves our attention. It is not great literature like *The Red Badge of*

Courage, and it did not have the profound effect on his career as did his Junior Mechanics article. But it's worth a look as Jersey-related entertainment. We're talking here about two articles on the subject of ghosts on the Jersey Shore that Crane churned out in his hungry freelance days, when he was earning five dollars a column. The first of the ghost articles appeared in the *New York Press* in November 1894; the second in January 1895.

The articles carried no byline, and the author was identified only as a "Special Correspondent." Except for a bit of literary detective work, we might never have known that they were written by the twenty-three-year-old Crane. It seems that his common-law wife, Cora, kept a scrapbook of her husband's work; after her death, the notebook was acquired by the Columbia University library, where it was examined by an expert on Crane, Professor Daniel G. Hoffman of Swarthmore. In the red scrapbook with its broken binding, the professor came across the ghost stories lovingly pasted in by Cora. On this basis, Professor Hoffman decided that the stories were Crane's, and they have since become a part of the collected works.

Professor Hoffman notes that there is nothing pathbreaking about these stories. Although they have the flavor of the Jersey Shore, they are inhabited by the stock plots and character types that were hackneyed even in the 1890s—the spirit of a fierce black dog guards his master's grave, an evil Indian hunts for the wife he murdered, a dead Tory captain weeps for the rebels he killed, a phantom pirate ship cruises the inlets, two ghostly lovers keep a tryst by the ocean.

What is pure Crane is the quality of the writing. Crane describes the violent surf as "a white smothering riot of water," a drowning sailor from a distance looks like "a black bead on this wild fabric of white foam," and a dog howls in the "indescribable key of woe." It also has about it Crane's pessimistic view of humans caught up in an uncaring universe.

Crane probably picked up some elements of his ghost stories from local folk along the Jersey Shore. Crane himself said that the area was filled with legends of the supernatural: "It can truly be said that more hair has risen on the New Jersey shore than any other known place."

The best of these stories was entitled by Crane "The Ghostly Sphynx of Metedeconk." Why the word *sphynx* (or *sphinx* in modern spelling)? Because in Greek mythology the Sphinx is a wrathful creature who asks questions of travelers.

But enough of this scholarly veneer; let us proceed to the story.

Around the year 1815, Crane tells us, a young maiden lived in a beautiful, flower-bedecked cottage by the ocean. The maiden was in love with a handsome sea captain. But one day the sailor came to announce that he was leaving on a long voyage to Buenos Aires. The maiden acted coldly, and the brokenhearted captain departed to his ship.

The maiden realized she had made a terrible mistake, but it was too late; her lover (in the old-fashioned sense of the word) had gone. As the days stretched on, she spent mournful hours on the beach, watching and waiting for a glimpse of her beloved's ship. "Her sorrow grew," wrote Crane, "and the fisherman used often to see her walking slowly back and forth, gazing eagerly into the southeast for the sail that would bear her lover to her." She grew thin and pale, with a feverish gleam in her large eyes.

Then one night a ferocious storm struck the coast. The maiden saw a sailing ship crash on the bar and break up under the lashing of the waves. Dead bodies washed up on the shore. One of those corpses was taken up by a wave and dashed at her feet; it was, of course, her sea captain, finally returned from his voyage.

And so, says Crane, this maiden became a ghost—"a moaning, mourning thing of the mist"—that haunted the beaches at night next to her ruined cottage. "It is claimed that when this phantom meets a human being face to face, she asks a question—a terrible, direct interrogation. She will ask concerning the body of her lover, who was drowned in 1815, and if the chattering mortal cannot at once give her an intelligent answer, containing terse information relating to the corpse, he is forthwith doomed, and his friends will find him next day lying pallid upon the shore."

To lend an air of credibility to his story, Crane tells of having spoken to a young fisherman who encountered the ghost along the beach. What follows are Crane's words.

"One night, when swift scudding clouds flew before the face of the moon, which was like a huge silver platter in the sky, the fisherman had occasion to pass this old house, with its battered sides, caving roof, and yard overgrown with brambles. The passing of the clouds before the moon made each somber shadow of the earth waver suggestively and the wind tossed the branches of the trees in strange and uncouth gestures. Within the house the old timbers creaked and moaned in a weird and low chant.

"By a desperate effort the fisherman dragged himself past the dark residence of the specter. Each wail of the old timbers was a voice that went to his soul, and each contortion of the shadows made by the wind-waved trees seemed to him to be the movement of a black and sinister figure creeping upon him.

"But it was when he was obliged to turn his back upon the old house that he suffered the most agony of mind. There was a little patch of flesh between his shoulder-blades that continually created the impression that a deathlike hand was about to be laid upon him. His trembling nerves told him that he was being approached by a mystic thing. He gave an involuntary cry and turned to look behind him.

"There stood the ghostly form of the white lady. Her hair fell in disheveled masses over her shoulders, her hands were clasped appealingly, and her large eyes gleamed with the one eternal and dread interrogation. Her lips parted and she was on the very verge of propounding the awful question, when the fisherman howled and started wildly for Metedeconk.

"There rang through the night the specter's cry of anger and despair, and the fisherman, although he was burdened with heavy boots, ran so fast that he fell from sheer exhaustion upon the threshold of his home. From that time forward it became habitual with him to wind up his lines when the sun was high over the pines of the western shore of Barnegat, and to reach his home before the chickens had gone to bed."

So ends Crane's story. If you ever happen to be walking alone along a Jersey beach some storm-tossed night and you feel your flesh creep, better not turn around.

23 Annie Oakley Lived in Nutley, New Jersey

The name Annie Oakley may not mean much to young people. A bunch of grade-school children interviewed by this writer had never heard of Annie Oakley or, for that matter, of Wild Bill Hickok, Wyatt Earp, Bat Masterson, or any of the other legendary heroes of the Old West.

But for those who grew up in earlier generations, Annie Oakley is a glamorous name from Broadway, the movies, and television. She was played by Ethel Merman in the hit musical *Annie Get Your Gun*. Betty Hutton and Barbara Stanwyck played the role in the movies. The blond, pigtailed actress Gail Davis portrayed Oakley in a popular television series.

So for those of us who regard Annie Oakley as a sort of mythical figure, the news that the real Oakley lived in Nutley is a bit startling, like learning that Wyatt Earp is buried in a Jewish cemetery near San Francisco or that Bat Masterson left the West to work as a sportswriter in New York. (Both true.)

The real Annie Oakley, in fact, was not a westerner at all. She was born well east of the Mississippi, on a farm in Ohio in 1860, and never saw a cowboy until later in life. Her real name was Annie Moses, and she was a brunette, not a blond. But she really was an expert markswoman, as much a natural athlete as Babe Ruth or Michael Jordan. She learned to handle a rifle as a child, and as a teenager was able to support her family by hunting game. She was so successful at local turkey shoots that she was banned from competing.

In her early twenties, she met Frank Butler, a professional marksman who performed on stage and in circuses. Butler was astonished by Oakley's shooting skill and won over by her charm. He abandoned his career to become her business manager, publicist, prop man—and husband.

He was able to get Annie hired by Buffalo Bill's Wild West show. Buffalo Bill (a.k.a. William F. Cody) was a former scout and buffalo hunter

Annie Oakley

When they weren't touring with Buffalo Bill's Wild West show, famed sharpshooter Annie Oakley and her husband, Frank Butler, resided in Nutley, New Jersey. Western History/Genealogy Department, Denver Public Library.

who, as much as anyone, was responsible for transforming the American West into an international myth. His popular show travelled from city to city, performing in outdoor arenas. It was a whooping, shooting, stampeding spectacular with cowboys, cavalrymen, Indians, stagecoaches, bison, and horses racing about in front of the awe-struck spectators.

Annie Oakley was a star of the Wild West show and a favorite of the crowds. The secret of her appeal was not just her shooting ability but her tremendous vitality. A petite woman, she would race into the arena in a girlish outfit of Western hat, blouse, leggings, and short (at least by nineteenth-century standards) skirt. For ten minutes she would fire furiously at clay birds and glass balls tossed in the air. She could hit the target facing backward with a mirror in her hand or while lying backward on a chair holding a shotgun upside down. She would leap over a table, grab a gun, whirl, and fire—smashing a target in the air before it hit the ground.

The appeal of "Little Sure Shot" reached well beyond America. When the Wild West show toured Europe, Oakley charmed celebrities like the president of France, the Prince of Wales, the emperor of Austria-Hungary, and Queen Victoria herself. Oakley shot the ashes off a cigarette held in the mouth of the Crown Prince of Prussia, who became Kaiser Wilhelm. In later years Annie joked that if her aim had been less accurate, the First World War might never have happened. The Indian chief Sitting Bull, who spent some time with the Wild West Show, was enamored of Oakley. The old warrior reportedly tried to adopt her as his daughter.

As Annie's fame grew, she and Frank decided to establish a permanent home. The Butlers had often visited New Jersey, competing in shooting matches in Newton, Dunellen, Merchantville, Long Branch, and elsewhere. But they fell in love with Nutley, which had a large and friendly colony of artists, writers, and performers. In December 1893, Mr. and Mrs. Frank Butler moved into a comfortable house built for them on Grant Avenue. It is said that the house was constructed without closets; after years of travelling, the Butlers were accustomed to living out of trunks.

Since the Wild West show spent most of the year on tour, the Butlers were in residence in Nutley mainly during the winter. But as much as any place in their lives, they regarded Nutley as their home, and they made lasting friends in the community. In 1894 Annie appeared in a local charity benefit. She stood on the back of a galloping horse, smashing glass balls with shots from her rifle.

Many writers have been fascinated by the image and reality of Annie Oakley. In an age when women were expected to be demure, protected, and passive, she projected an appealing, even daring, aura of energy, skill, and athleticism. By triumphing in the man's world of sharpshooting, she helped to stretch the sphere of women. In her private life, though, Annie was staunchly conservative. She fixed her costume so it would not display an undue amount of leg, and years later, on her death bed, she insisted that her body be turned over to a female embalmer.

She and Frank Butler had a remarkably loving marriage. He called her Missie; she called him Jimmie. They kept voluminous scrapbooks of their travels together, and he would write romantic poems to her. They shared a love of shooting, and were friendly with sportspeople around the United States.

They also shared a lifelong interest in pinching pennies, which perhaps can be explained by their backgrounds. Frank came to the United States as a destitute Irish immigrant; Annie's family in Ohio went through a long stretch of grinding poverty, and she spent part of her childhood on the county poor farm.

The Wild West show made Annie world famous and wealthy, and the Butlers probably would have continued for many more seasons. But in 1901, Annie was injured in a train accident. She retired from the show after having performed as Little Sure Shot for sixteen years.

She continued to work for a time as the star of a melodrama, *The Western Girl*, and still later made a short tour with another traveling Western show. But by this time she was middle aged. Although she still wore the same little-girl costume, she needed a wig to cover her gray hair.

The Butlers sold their Nutley home in 1904. For a brief period they lived in an apartment in East Orange and then moved to a retirement home in the South.

The last years were mostly pleasant. Annie continued to make personal appearances and demonstrate her marksmanship; among other feats, she would shoot an apple off the head of her pet dog. Even after a 1922 automobile accident left her permanently crippled, she was able to shoot coins tossed in the air. She died at age sixty-six in 1926; Frank died eighteen days after his beloved wife.

All of this is not exactly like the story of Annie Oakley presented by Broadway and Hollywood, but the real story of her life is about as colorful and satisfying as it gets in our world.

24  Scandal at the Girls' Reform School

Back in the 1890s, a New York newspaper discovered a way to add a splash of color to the comics pages by using yellow ink, and so the "yellow press" was born. But the term came to stand for more than just a printing gimmick; it was used to describe a sensationalistic journalistic style of screaming headlines and slashing articles, in which the press took on the role of defender of the public against evil.

You could say this for yellow journalism—it sure sold newspapers. The circulation of some big-city papers soared into the hundreds of thousands. So it was inevitable that local papers outside the big cities adopted the same crusading tone of voice, although not the yellow ink.

All of which sets the stage for a noisy turn-of-the century struggle that pitted the newspapers against Mrs. Myrtle B. Eyler, the matron of the New Jersey State Industrial School for Girls.

Located outside Trenton, the Girls' School was a reformatory for females age seven to twenty-one who were guilty of a crime or who, in the words of the law, were found to be "habitually disorderly, incorrigible, or vagrant." A staff of twenty under the supervision of Matron Eyler instructed the 130 inmates in cooking, baking, sewing, and farm work in order to turn them into useful citizens.

In the summer of 1899, rumors of abuses at the school began to appear in the press. One inmate who had been admitted to a Trenton hospital suffering from exhaustion told a shocking story: she said that as punishment for breaking the rules she had been forced to run repeatedly up and down a forty-foot flight of stairs and was then locked up in a basement room and fed on bread and water.

The newspapers put pressure on Governor Foster M. Voorhees to investigate the matter. Trailed by reporters, the governor made the two-mile carriage ride from the state capitol building to the school. He got an earful. Unhappy staff members testified that Matron Eyler used harsh discipline on the inmates. Witnesses told the governor it was common for Mrs. Eyler to have rebellious girls locked into an unventilated room in the basement known as the "dungeon." Sometimes the girls were shackled and placed in straitjackets.

Cooking Class
This uplifting photo of inmates at the New Jersey State Industrial School for Girls learning a useful skill dates from the year 1900; it was at about this time that the press was ablaze with allegations of brutal beatings and starvation at the institution. How much of this did the women in the picture know? What were they thinking as they posed for the camera? New Jersey State Archives, Department of State.

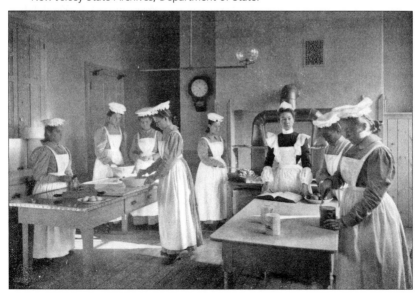

But that was not the worst. Staff members said that Matron Eyler frequently administered beatings and whippings. The janitor and the coachman described how on one occasion they held a screaming girl to a chair while Mrs. Eyler pulled the victim's head backward by the hair and repeatedly slapped her face. The girl's crime, according to the janitor, had been to refuse to answer a question put to her by the matron.

When one inmate refused to plant potatoes because she was sick, Mrs. Eyler reportedly beat her with a strap as the girl was dragged to the field by a farmhand. Witnesses said that as she struck the girls, Mrs. Eyler would yell: "You got the devil in you, and I'm going to get it out of you." It was alleged that Mrs. Eyler had fired staff members who opposed her and filled their places with relatives and friends. Her husband, Clarence, was the school clerk.

The press reported all this in lurid detail. "Inmates Cruelly Lashed—Shocking Testimony at the Investigation of a Trenton School" ran a typical headline. The loudest critic of Mrs. Eyler was the *Trenton Times*, which painted the matron as a sadistic, twisted caricature of a human being and demanded her dismissal.

The scandal broke not long after the patriotic frenzy of the American war with Spain. One of the principal villains of the war had been General Valeriano Weyler, the Spanish governor of Cuba. "Butcher" Weyler was reviled in the yellow press for setting up concentration camps in Cuba where innocent women and children were starved and tortured. A cynical Trenton reporter, William Sackett, observed years later that the newspapers seized on the Matron Eyler story in large part because her name was so close to Butcher Weyler's. It was as if a modern-day suspect in a child-abuse case was named bin Laden.

And so the press, led by the *Trenton Times*, fanned public outrage against the evil Mrs. Eyler and her house of horrors in Ewing Township. The inmates themselves enthusiastically followed the exposé. A mother sent her inmate daughter a cake with newspaper clippings stuffed inside.

But Mrs. Eyler had her supporters. The *Trenton True American*, a rival of the *Times*, defended the matron on the grounds that the reformatory was not a finishing school for refined young ladies but a penal institution that housed a vicious and depraved population.

Mrs. Eyler herself said that some of the charges against her were exaggerations and that others were outright lies by her enemies on the staff. She pointed to the reforms she had made at the school. She had built playgrounds and reading rooms for the girls, and she took away the tight corsets the girls had been required to wear and replaced them with looser, more modern undergarments.

But she never denied that she believed in discipline. She said the young women were there because they had never learned to obey, and it was her job to teach that obedience. She wrote: "To restrain and correct that which is evil in its nature and influence, some discipline is necessary."

Governor Voorhees was convinced that Mrs. Eyler had acted properly to maintain order and that her newspaper critics were a bunch of busybodies. A Mercer County grand jury that investigated the case refused to return a bill against her. A probe by the Society for the Prevention of Cruelty to Children got nowhere, and a lawsuit by a former inmate fizzled. The trustees of the school threatened to sue the *Trenton Times* for libel.

But the *Times* refused to quit. The paper sponsored a petition drive demanding an investigation by the legislature. Prodded by the *Times*, newspapers around the state joined in the call. When the state Assembly finally appointed a committee for that purpose, the *Trenton Times* patted itself on the back in a front-page story, boasting that the paper had trounced the special interests and brought Matron Eyler to justice.

The Assembly committee issued a report recommending improvements in the management of the reformatory. But except for changing the name from "The State Industrial School for Girls" to "The State Home for Girls," nothing much happened. Mrs. Eyler remained in charge and was in fact promoted to the position of superintendent as a demonstration of the trustees' support.

"Shame! Shame! Shame!" cried the editorial in the *Trenton Times*, about the way in which Mrs. Eyler was shielded from the wrath of the people.

The *Times* continued to hammer away at the story, until finally a newly elected governor, Franklin Murphy, could stand the outcry no longer. He forced the trustees of the Girls' School to resign, and the new board of trustees promptly fired Mrs. Eyler and six of her relatives and friends.

The scandal had lasted for five years, but Matron Eyler had finally been vanquished by the press. The triumphant title of a *Trenton Times* editorial said it all: "At Last."

25  Alice Goes for a Drive

Some feminists look down their noses at "famous firsts": the first woman astronaut, the first woman to swim the English Channel, the first woman senator, and so forth. And maybe it is a bit condescending to look at women's history as just a game of catch-up.

But what the heck, Alice Huyler Ramsey was an appealing, self-possessed, competent New Jersey woman who deserves to be remembered for her famous first: back in the summer of 1909, the twenty-two-year-old Ramsey became the first woman to drive an automobile from coast to coast.

Ramsey was the young wife of a well-to-do Hackensack attorney. She could have lived a life of ease, but she had a taste for adventure. To indulge his wife—and to keep her from riding horses, which he thought too dangerous, her husband bought her a new Maxwell automobile. This was just before the age of the mass-produced Model T, and cars were still exotic and expensive toys. Ramsey proved to be an excellent motorist and an ace mechanic. In rallies and long-distance trips, she established a reputation as one of the best drivers in the Northeast.

A sales manager from the Maxwell company was struck with a public relations inspiration: why not have the plucky woman drive a Maxwell from New York City to San Francisco? When the Maxwell man proposed the idea, Ramsey was embarrassed: "My face felt like a fireball, and I would gladly have disappeared under the table," she recalled. But the

Alice Huyler Ramsey
In 1909, the plucky, twenty-two-year-old Alice Ramsey of Hackensack
became the first woman to drive an automobile from coast to coast.
Special Collections and University Archives, Rutgers University Libraries—
Women's Project of New Jersey Collection.

more she thought about it, the more enthusiastic she became. She
decided to take the challenge and to take along as chaperones three companions who had been passengers with her before: her sisters-in-law and
an unmarried female friend from Hackensack. This being 1909, Ramsey
had to obtain her husband's permission.

The Maxwell company supplied the car and paid expenses. Maxwell
agents on the route were instructed to help by providing guidance through
unfamiliar territory. An advance man was hired to precede her by train
from town to town, to handle publicity and make hotel accommodations.

But it was still a perilous undertaking. Outside of a few big cities,
there were virtually no paved roads in the nation and no road maps.
Much of the country was still unsettled, and friends advised Ramsey to
take a gun along. (She decided not to.)

By modern standards the car was primitive. It was a four-cylinder, 30-horsepower vehicle, with a top speed of forty miles an hour. The crank had to be turned to start the ignition. The tires had no treads. A pull-down canvas top was the only protection against rain and dust. The gas gauge consisted of a wooden ruler that had to be dipped into the gas tank to check the level. The headlamps were started by dropping a pellet in water to generate gas that was then ignited with a match. The car had little storage space, so luggage, spare tires, tire chains, water, and tools had to be lashed on the back and running board.

On a rainy June 9, Ramsey and her companions began the trip from the Maxwell headquarters in Manhattan. The first leg, from New York to Chicago, was relatively easy by the standards of 1909. On a good day Ramsey was able to make over 130 miles on the bumpy and dusty roads, reaching Chicago in fourteen days.

But conditions deteriorated once she crossed the Mississippi. The roads were hardly roads at all in any sense we would recognize: sometimes they were wagon ruts through the sagebrush; other times they were rain-soaked mudflats. Ramsey became an expert on holes: mud holes, chuck holes, prairie-dog holes, arroyos. Sometimes the car had to be towed out by horses; three times it broke an axle. It took thirteen days of rough driving to make it just across Iowa.

In Wyoming Ramsey found that the bridge over the Platte River had been washed away, so she had to drive the car along an open railroad trestle twenty feet over the river. As she bumped along she worried about breaking an axle on the railroad ties, falling off the edge, getting stuck from loss of momentum, or being hit by a locomotive. "It was one of those places where you don't look down—you keep plowing steadily on," she recalled.

Ramsey did all of the driving and most of the repair work. She fixed flat tires, took apart and cleaned spark plugs, helped replace axles, scrapped cylinder heads, and tightened loose bolts. In Nebraska, she crawled underneath the car to fix the brake pedal with wire. "I was born mechanical," she said with pride.

The conditions were primitive. In Iowa she had to sleep in the car when the road was blocked by a swollen river; after seventeen straight hours of driving, in Utah she caught some sleep at 3:00 in the morning, on the ground beside her car. At a rundown hotel in Wyoming, she woke up to find her bed was crawling with bugs, and went to sleep in the lobby.

Near the Rocky Mountains her car was stopped by a grim-faced posse searching for a murderer. In Nevada, Indians brandishing bows and arrows galloped past.

But she approached everything with a sense of enthusiasm and a taste for adventure. She played the piano at a restaurant in Iowa and went horseback riding in Wyoming. She admired the scenery, and was amused when she was served a predawn breakfast of lamb chops and chocolate cake in Nevada. She enjoyed the amazement caused by her New Jersey license plates.

Her sisters-in-law seemed to have a great deal less enthusiasm. Ramsey had to talk them out of taking pillows along on the trip. They did manage to take cut-crystal glasses with silver tops, which they wound up using to fill the radiator with water from roadside ditches to prevent overheating. Disgusted by the jolting ride and the choking dust, from time to time the sisters left the car to travel by train.

The forty-one-day, thirty-eight-hundred-mile trip ended with a difficult but breathtaking ride up over the mighty Sierra Nevadas and down into San Francisco, where Ramsey was welcomed by enthusiastic crowds and honking horns. But she didn't remain there long; she returned home as soon as she could (by train) for a joyous reunion with her husband. We know it was joyous because she had a baby nine months later.

Ramsey continued to drive from coast to coast well into her seventies. She died in 1983 at age ninety-seven.

One could not call Alice Ramsey a crusading feminist. But there was a revealing moment at an Iowa crossroads, when she came across a farm woman sitting alone in a wagon hitched to a team of horses. "Are you the women who are driving from New York to San Francisco?" asked the farm woman.

"Yes we are," replied Alice.

"I'm sure glad. I read about you in the paper and I've come six miles to see you and I've been waiting for a long time. Yes, I'm sure glad I saw you!"

It was a striking encounter between two self-reliant women, and Alice Ramsey remembered the moment for the rest of her life.

26  Billy Sunday Came to Trenton on Monday

Billy Sunday was his real name, and he was America's most famous preacher, bigger than all the modern television evangelists put together. And on a Monday in 1915, Sunday came to New Jersey to bring the word of God to the state legislature.

In his youth, the Iowa-born Billy Sunday was a popular outfielder for the Chicago White Stockings baseball team. While making the rounds of Chicago bars with his teammates one night in 1886, he paused to listen to a missionary band playing hymns on the street corner. He followed the band to a storefront mission and before long was won over to Christ. Billy Sunday quit stealing bases and started saving souls, traveling the countryside as an itinerant minister.

He brought to the revival trail a powerful stage presence that, together with his fame as a former baseball star, carried him to the top rank of evangelists. His appearances attracted thousands of followers. Wealthy men like the millionaire John D. Rockefeller bankrolled Sunday's campaigns, and the evangelist appeared in small towns and big cities across the nation.

A Billy Sunday performance was something to behold. Pouring sweat and with the veins in his neck bulging, the muscular preacher would leap about the stage, jump up on tables, punch the air with his fist, and smash chairs to smite the devil.

He was a fundamentalist who believed in the literal truth of the Bible. He was against sin, of course, but against much of the modern world as well, including what he believed were wicked foreign philosophies like evolution, psychology, birth control, atheism, and socialism. He assured his faithful that Darwin, Galileo, and Plato were all in Hell. He was one of the leading voices in the nation for a total ban on alcohol.

In 1915, when he was at the height of his fame, the fifty-two-year-old preacher was holding a revival in Philadelphia when some members of the New Jersey legislature invited him to cross the Delaware to Trenton to speak in the State House on Monday, March 15.

New Jersey in those years was changing from the rural, old-time Protestant America that Billy Sunday represented. It was a state with growing cities, filled with foreigners. More than half the people of the state were immigrants or their children. City folk outnumbered farmers by more than two to one. Party bosses and lobbyists from saloons and other special interests played a powerful role in state government.

But Trenton turned out for Billy Sunday. A crowd estimated in the thousands waited for hours outside the State House to see him. Some of Sunday's fans outside climbed on the ledge of the State House to peer through the window. Inside, the Assembly chamber was filled to its maximum capacity of four hundred. Every seat in the galleries and on the floor was filled. In the audience were senators, assemblymen, reporters, State House janitors, and members of the public, as well as Governor James Fielder. The business of the government was adjourned for the day.

Billy arrived at the State House that afternoon in a limousine donated by the Philadelphia department store magnate John Wanamaker. The evangelist flashed his famous smile and waved as he emerged from the car, accompanied by his well-known wife, Helen "Ma" Sunday. A delegation of legislators led the Sundays into the Assembly chamber. Once inside, the Speaker of the Assembly and the president of the Senate turned over the chamber to Billy. The evangelist's musical director, Homer Rodeheaver, warmed up the audience by leading them in the hymn "Brighten the Corner," accompanied by a trumpet and portable organ. Then the master himself stepped up to the Assembly Speaker's desk. The evangelist had a repertoire of hard-hitting sermons that he delivered from memory, and for his Trenton audience he selected one of the favorites, "Man or Mutt, Gasoline or Dishwater, Heads or Tails."

The sermon was based on the Old Testament passage in 1 Kings 2:2, "Be thou strong and show thyself a man." Sunday's message was that his listeners should shun sin and weakness to live a life of "manliness," as he termed it in those politically incorrect days. "Be a man," he exhorted the audience, "not a frame to hang clothes on." (The large contingent of women in the audience did not seem to object to the masculine theme.)

He cited examples of manliness from the Bible, using his trademark slangy language. He described how David took on Goliath: "When the fight was on and Goliath was making his usual spiel, David trots along and says, 'Who's that lobster out there putting up that game of talk?'" And then: "David just took that sling, whirled it around and soaked him on the coco between the lamps and the giant went to the mat and took the count."

The speech was flavored with other Billy Sundayisms. "A dead fish can float, but it takes a live one to wriggle upstream." "Don't look for an easy chair or a cushion if you want to hang your mug in God's hall of fame." "A mockingbird will never learn to sing if he takes music lessons from a crow or a hoot owl."

"There's a call all over this country for strong Christian men," cried Sunday. "If it pleases God, be a man, not a mutt!"

Sunday had a special word for the politicians seated before him. "Stand up, you God-forsaken, hog-jowled, peanut-brained ward heelers, grafting politicians, and see how a man can be a man!" A reporter for the *New York Herald* heard a "suppressed gasp" from the audience at those words.

All of this he delivered with his famous brand of stage energy and emotion. At one point the evangelist leaped up on the desk of the Speaker of the Assembly; at another he punched the air with his fist a few feet from the face of Governor Fielder.

But Sunday did exercise restraint on one subject. He was aware that the legislature was in the midst of a debate over a bill allowing towns to ban saloons. So while he expressed scorn for drink and drunkards, he left out the more extreme Prohibition diatribe that was a standard part of his "Man or Mutt" sermon. This caused some embarrassment to the *Trenton Times*, which, in its haste to make the evening edition, reprinted the speech before it was actually delivered, including the extreme temperance parts.

A reporter thought that because of the sophistication of the legislators, it took them a while to warm up to Sunday. But twenty minutes into the sermon they were cheering, clapping, and whistling.

When it was over, the legislators publicly thanked Sunday and presented him with an elaborate floral horseshoe, in the center of which was the state seal. The horseshoe was so big that after it was loaded in the limousine it was difficult for Billy and Ma to squeeze in.

So ended this encounter between church and state. There is no evidence that Billy Sunday fell into debauchery for having been in New Jersey, or that the Garden State became more godly because of his presence. A few days later, as expected, the Assembly resoundingly voted down the antisaloon bill.

27  Ezra Pound Insults Newark

The year 1916 was Newark's 250th anniversary, and the city put on pageants and parades to celebrate itself. As part of the festivities, the city fathers decided to hold a poetry contest. A prize committee was appointed, consisting of the mayor, a circuit judge, a Rutgers art history professor, a high school English teacher, a literary editor, and a poet.

The judges proclaimed that they were looking for a poem that would celebrate Newark: "We think our city already quite worthy," said the announcement. "Now we seek a poet who shall make us famous!" A Newark magazine merrily published a rhyming invitation: "Come all ye poets, great and small, / Ye little fat ones and ye tall." One thousand dollars was set aside for prizes: $250 for first place, $150 second, $100 third, and ten runner-up prizes of $10 each.

Now the scene shifts from joyous Newark, New Jersey, to the flat of the thirty-year-old Ezra Pound in beleaguered wartime London, England.

Pound was an American who grew up in Pennsylvania. He was an occasional visitor to New Jersey, and in fact had a youthful romance with a Miss Mary Moore of Trenton. He came to find the puritanical atmosphere of his native country stifling, and in 1908 he left the United States to live the bohemian life in Europe.

Pound became a well-known figure in the London avant-garde, writing a bold, vigorous new poetry that cast aside Victorian prudery. He delighted in shocking the bourgeoisie. "You funghus," he addressed readers in one poem, "you continuous gangrene." His physical appearance itself was designed to defy convention: he strode London with a shock of reddish blond hair, an outfit of green trousers and pink velvet coat, and (shocking at least in that era) a solitary earring.

But there were drawbacks to living one's life as a rebuke to comfortable society. The poems and reviews he wrote for obscure literary journals paid little, and he was constantly in need of cash. With the outbreak of World War I, life in London became harsh for Pound and his fellow literary rebels. Somehow he received an announcement of the Newark poetry competition. The brash civic boosterism of the announcement intrigued him, but even more appealing with the possibility of $250. He sat down and wrote a poem he entitled "To a City Sending Him Advertisements."

The poem speaks sarcastically of American cities like Newark, devoted to commerce: "Careless of all that's quiet, / Seeing the flare, the glitter only." How different from the ancient, graceful cities of Italy, "each with form, light, character." These cities had been made beautiful and orderly by the tyrants of the Renaissance. Could the democracy of Newark—"your demos," Pound called it—ever match that beauty and order? Could any of Newark's hundreds of thousands of citizens ever look beyond their crass, ordinary lives to see something nobler?

No, Pound concluded, Newark could not. He took a swipe at the "professors, mayors, judges" who made up the prize committee. Their purpose, he wrote, was merely to "implant a soul in your tick of commerce." He predicted they would give the award to a more flattering poet:

> Some more loud-mouthed fellow,
>   slamming a bigger drum,
> Some fellow rhyming and roaring,
> Some more obsequious hack.

A central figure in the poem is Apollo, the Greek god who represents both beauty and destruction. Pound warned that if Newark did not reach for beauty, for "the silvery heel of Apollo," then it would be crushed by that heel.

When this somber, difficult poem arrived in Newark as one of the nine hundred entries, the judges were shocked. They wrote that Pound "assaulted our civic sensibilities in a poem of violence directed at the head, heart, and hands of Newark." One member of the panel voted against it; another pronounced it "captious, arrogant, hypercritical." The committee sarcastically referred to Pound as a "philosophic iconoclast" and an "exponent of Imagist School of Poetic Palpitation."

But the committee nevertheless decided to award Pound a ten-dollar runner-up prize, and to publish his work along with the other winning poems. "There is food for thought in our London poet's catechistic cadences," the committee members conceded. "Let us not begrudge him the high appraisal of our poetry judges."

Pound was utterly correct about the sort of poem that would win the top prize. Written by one Clement Wood, it was a rhyming, roaring hymn to Newark, filled with praise:

> And out of the smothering din and grime
> I forge a city for all time;
> A city beautiful and clean,
> With wide sweet avenues of green,
> With gracious homes and houses of trade,
> Where souls as well as things are made.

Pound was pleased by his ten dollars, if a bit peeved that it took so long to arrive.

After the war, Pound left England to live first in France and then in Italy. He was a friend of Gertrude Stein, T. S. Eliot, Ernest Hemingway, and other luminaries of the avant-garde. His work, especially his long poem *The Cantos*, brought him international fame.

But there was more to Pound than poetry. He was deeply alienated, like many of his generation who lived through the bloodbath of World War I. He likened the modern world to "an old bitch gone in the teeth . . . a botched civilization." The impatience with crass democracy and the admiration for enlightened tyrants evident in his Newark poem became an obsession. He spoke bitterly of the "syphilis of capitalism." Like many who hate democracy and the modern world, he became a virulent anti-Semite.

Pound admired Hitler, but he found his ideal of the enlightened tyrant in Mussolini, the fascist dictator of Italy. He obtained an audience with Il Duce in 1933 and gushed when he saw that the dictator had a volume of *The Cantos* on his desk. He saw Mussolini as a man who would allow the arts to flourish and who would create an organic social order, far superior to the chaos of capitalist democracy.

When World War II erupted, Pound made regular broadcasts from Italy defending Fascism and attacking "Franklin Finkelstein Roosevelt" and other "war pimps" like Churchill. In one broadcast he ranted: "Every human being who is not a hopeless idiotic worm should realize that fascism is superior in every way to Russian Jewocracy and that capitalism stinks."

When the war ended he was brought back to America under arrest and placed on trial for treason. He was judged legally insane and spent twelve years in a Washington, D.C., lunatic asylum. After his release he returned to Italy to live out his remaining years. He died in Venice in 1972 at age eighty-seven, a morose, defeated man.

Those of a poetic bent can perhaps read significance into all this. Maybe those self-confident, comfortable burghers of Newark in 1916 did not deserve the scorn heaped on them by Ezra Pound. Maybe living in a decent, democratic society is not such a blind and ignoble way to make one's way through life after all.

28 Cher Ami

After the end of World War I, a scarred survivor of the Western Front came to Fort Monmouth, New Jersey. The veteran had lost a leg in air combat and had been honored by General John Pershing for saving hundreds of American lives. When this hero died, in June 1919, its body was stuffed by a taxidermist and placed on display in the Smithsonian, where it can be seen today.

As the reader may have guessed by now, we're talking pigeons, not people. The veteran was U.S. Army pigeon number NURP-18–615, known familiarly as "Cher Ami." There is some confusion about Cher Ami's gender. The Signal Corps records of World War I list NURP-18–615 as a blue check hen. But the standard reference work *The Pigeon* by Wendell Levi, a former president of the National Pigeon Association, describes Cher Ami as a blue check cock. It's this sort of thing that makes people skeptical of history. For the sake of gender equity, we will treat her as female.

Carrier pigeons, or "racing homers," have been used to carry messages in wartime for thousands of years. They don't have wires that can break, batteries that can run down, or broadcasts that can be overheard. Plus, they basically work for chicken feed.

World War I brought the United States into the pigeon business in a big way. Within a few months of American entry into the war, the Signal Corps established training and breeding centers at Fort Monmouth and elsewhere and invented portable lofts that could be moved quickly around the front. By the time the Great War was over, fifteen thousand pigeons were in American uniform, so to speak. (The uniform consisted of a metal leg band stamped with the serial number.)

Cher Ami was one of five hundred pigeons given by the British to the American Expeditionary Force for use on the Western Front. Her moment of glory came during the Argonne forest offensive in October

Cher Ami
This heroic pigeon, Cher Ami, is credited with saving American soldiers
in World War I. After the war, the bird lived at Fort Monmouth,
New Jersey; its stuffed body is now on display in the Smithsonian.
Courtesy of the Smithsonian Institution, photographer Jeff Tinsley.

1918. A battalion of the Seventy-seventh Division moving in advance of
the rest of the army was cut off and surrounded by German troops.
Enemy machine-gun fire, mortars, and hand grenades rained in on the
battalion. Even worse, the battalion was being devastated by the friendly
fire of American artillery. Other pigeons sent out by the battalion were
shot out of the sky.

Then Cher Ami was released (or liberated, to use the appealing
technical term) with a message in a tube attached to her leg: "We are

along the road parallel 276.4. Our own artillery is dropping a barrage directly on us. For heaven's sake, stop it." The bird paused on a branch to preen itself until a doughboy climbed the tree and shooed her into the air.

Cher Ami made the forty-kilometer trip to her roost at division headquarters in twenty-five minutes. When she arrived, it was found that a piece of shrapnel had cut off her leg and penetrated her chest—the message tube dangled by a tendon. But the communication got through and the artillery barrage was lifted. A short time later, the Lost Battalion, as it came to be called, was rescued.

After the war, Cher Ami was brought to the Signal Corps center at Fort Monmouth, along with other celebrated pigeon survivors of the war. One of them was "President Wilson," who also lost a leg on the Western Front and who is today on display next to Cher Ami in the Smithsonian. Another was "The Mocker," who lost an eye and the top of his head but who lived for twenty years after the war and whose carcass was for many years exhibited in the post library.

"G.I. Joe," a celebrated pigeon of World War II, was a later retiree at Fort Monmouth. He is credited with saving a thousand troops on the Italian front in 1943 by bringing the message that a town that the Allies were about to bomb was occupied by British infantry. He was presented with a medal by the Lord Mayor of London.

But of all the pigeon veterans, it was Cher Ami who became the most famous. Children's author Marion B. Cothren wrote a popular book, *Cher Ami, The Story of a Carrier Pigeon*, which helped make the bird an American war hero like ace aviator Captain Eddie Rickenbaker and the brave infantryman Sergeant Alvin York.

How do pigeons like Cher Ami manage to return unerringly to their lofts, even when they are transported hundreds of miles from home? All sorts of theories have been advanced. Maybe they use the sun to navigate, or the Earth's magnetic field, or the the sense of smell, or the direction of the winds. Maybe they can somehow keep track of the twists and turns made by the vehicles that take them away from their roosts.

Scientists have gone to great lengths to test out these various theories. In separate experiments, pigeons have been: strapped with electrically charged coils to disrupt magnetism; fitted with tiny contact lenses to block out the sun; anesthetized to take away their sense of smell; tricked by deflecting panels that distort the wind's direction; and knocked out with drugs to prevent them from memorizing the route they are trucked. To disrupt their internal clock, they have been kept indoors and subjected to artificial day and night.

But, so far, the pigeons with their tiny brains have been able to outwit the scientists with their big ones. No matter what measures are taken, the birds generally make their way home. The accepted explanation at present is that pigeons use several different tools. On a clear day they reckon direction by using the sun; on a cloudy day, the Earth's magnetism. Inside each pigeon's head there seems to be a "compass" that indicates direction and a "map" that recognizes the terrain.

So pigeons turn out to be pretty smart little critters. But maybe we go a bit too far when we ascribe human qualities to them. Can we really say, as her admirers do, that Cher Ami was brave and heroic? Homing pigeons have been bred for generations for one quality—to flap their wings like mad and scoot toward home. It is not as if Cher Ami had the option of surrendering to the Germans, or losing herself in the civilian bird population. If she kept on flying after being wounded, it had more to do with genetic programming than with a desire to make the world safe for democracy.

But we can still respect Cher Ami and the other wartime pigeons. They were stuffed into tiny cages and carried about on the backs of infantrymen or in noisy trucks, biplanes, and tanks, then liberated into the air to be shot at by rifles and machine guns—all for the mysterious purposes of us higher creatures.

And while we humans can today admire old NURP-18–625 inside the Smithsonian Air and Space Museum, the pigeons who peck at discarded snack food and annoy tourists on the mall outside the museum are blithely unaware of their famous sister (or maybe brother) enshrined inside.

29  The Poet, the Athlete, and the War to End All Wars

Few people are still alive who remember World War I. The Armistice Day holiday that was meant to commemorate the end of that war has become the generic Veteran's Day, which for most of us is just an occasion for a shopping trip to the mall. But it's worth reflecting on that first of the world wars, and how it shattered the ideals of a generation.

Consider two New Jerseyans who went off to World War I, two out of the millions who fought. One was a man of the mind, a poet and literary figure. The other was an athlete, a hero of the arena and stadium.

Joyce Kilmer was born and raised in New Brunswick, New Jersey. His parents gave him the name Joyce in honor of the local Episcopal rector, Elisha Joyce—thus confusing generations of readers about the poet's gender. He attended Rutgers College for two years, but he had trouble with the mathematics requirement and then transferred to Columbia. After graduation he entered the literary world of New York where, among other pursuits, he wrote book reviews for the *New York Times*.

Kilmer is best remembered as the author of the 1913 "Trees" ("I think that I shall never see . . ."). That poem made him famous and has been read around the world and set to music. But he wrote hundreds of other popular poems, along with essays, lectures, book reviews, and articles.

Kilmer did not even remotely fit the stereotype of the starving, alienated poet. He was an enthusiastic eater, a bit on the pudgy side. He was profoundly in love with his wife, and they lived together in a happy suburban home in Mahwah, filled with their children and their friends. He was deeply religious, and he and his wife converted to Catholicism.

Kilmer's poems are optimistic, upbeat celebrations of home, family, and God's creation. They typically begin with something ordinary, like a tree, and then soar upward to larger themes. A friend once challenged Kilmer to write about the most mundane subject imaginable—

Joyce Kilmer
When the United States entered World War I, Kilmer, famous for his poem "Trees," enlisted in the army. He died in battle on the Western Front in 1918. Special Collections and University Archives, Rutgers University Libraries—R-BIO Collection.

a delicatessen. The poem that Kilmer composed, "Delicatessen," portrays a store owner who lives in a dreary world of sliced cheese and pickles, but "This man has home and child and wife. . . . This man has God and love and life." The poem concludes: "Have pity on our foolishness / And give us eyes that we may see / Beneath the shopman's clumsy dress / The splendour of humanity!"

Another poem, "The Twelve-forty-five," describes the late-night train he would sometimes take from Manhattan to Mahwah, with details of the station waiting room and the Jersey towns he passed through in the dark, and his arrival home: "My cottage lamp shines white and clear. / God bless the train that brought me here."

Where Kilmer became famous because of his ability with words and rhymes, Hobart "Hobey" Baker achieved fame from his skill with a football and a hockey stick. Baker came from a well-to-do Philadelphia family with ties to New Jersey. He attended Princeton, class of 1914, where he became the most famous college athlete of his day.

Hobey Baker excelled at every sport—tennis, baseball, golf, diving, swimming—but he was best known at Princeton as a star of the gridiron. Thousands of spectators would come to watch him run the ball relentlessly downfield, brilliantly outmaneuvering the opposition to score touchdowns. A Boston newspaper described Baker as "the most feared open field runner now playing the game of football."

It was the same in hockey, in those days a popular varsity sport. Baker would streak down the ice, eluding opponents, and smashing in goals. The press called him "the greatest amateur hockey player ever developed in this country or Canada."

The blond, handsome Baker, five feet, nine inches tall, 160 pounds, was an extraordinary athlete. His biographer, John Davies, says of Baker, "He had a great physique, fantastic reflexes, instant coordination of hand and eye, iron discipline, blazing courage." He was also polite and modest. He blushed when signs were posted at arenas saying "Hobey Baker Plays Tonight." He played for the sheer joy of sport and was proud of observing the rules of the game and respecting his opponents. He disdainfully referred to those who cheated or committed willful fouls as "muckers." F. Scott Fitzgerald knew Baker at Princeton and said of him that he was "an ideal worthy of everything in my enthusiastic admiration."

We don't know if Joyce Kilmer and Hobey Baker ever met. But the two young men shared the same sense of optimism and morality. It's not unlikely that Baker read and admired "Trees" and that Kilmer was one of the fans who came to watch the Princeton champion.

When America entered the World War in 1917, the poet Kilmer and the athlete Baker both immediately volunteered. Kilmer wound up as a sergeant in the Forty-third Rainbow Division in France, attached (as befitting a man of the mind) to the intelligence unit. He enjoyed soldiering. In a letter from France he wrote about his fellow infantrymen, "Danger shared together and hardships mutually borne develops in us a sort of friendship I never knew in civilian life."

In late July 1918, Kilmer's division was thrown against the German lines. He was found dead on the battlefield, with a bullet through his thoughtful, optimistic brain. He was thirty-one years old.

The athlete Hobey Baker went into the Air Corps, where he delighted in swooping and wheeling through the air. He wrote home: "You handle your machine instinctively just as you dodge instinctively when running with the ball in an open field." He was credited with downing three German planes, and late in the war he was given command of a new American air squadron. The squadron's planes were painted in Princeton orange and black and decorated with an emblem of the Princeton tiger.

On December 21, forty days after the armistice, Baker decided to take a Spad airplane up for one last flight before leaving the squadron to return to America. The engine failed, and the plane smashed into the ground, crushing his athletic body. He died in the ambulance taking him from the wreck. He was twenty-six years old.

The devastation and death of World War I helped to spread a great feeling of alienation and cynicism among those who survived. For the generation that went to war, the old words like glory, honor, and courage seemed obscene after the slaughter they had witnessed. Sentimental, idealistic poems like "Trees" came to be regarded as hopelessly old-fashioned and saccharine. The most celebrated work of poetry of the postwar era was T. S. Eliot's 1922 "The Waste Land," a despairing portrait of a godless, materialistic world—about as far from the sunny poems of Joyce Kilmer as one could imagine.

That same sense of cynicism pervaded the big-money world of professional sports that emerged after the war. In the 1919 World Series, baseball players took bribes from gamblers to throw the series, as far from the good sportsmanship of Hobey Baker as one could imagine. The muckers had triumphed.

The war that killed Hobey Baker and Joyce Kilmer destroyed their world as well.

30  The Applejack Campaign

The feisty gubernatorial election of 1919 was a classic New Jersey political battle that has been known ever since as the "Applejack Campaign," after New Jersey's native alcoholic beverage.

It was a contest between the Prohibitionist "drys" and the anti-Prohibition "wets." The Eighteenth Amendment to the Constitution had been ratified, and beginning in the New Year, the manufacture or sale of intoxicating liquor was to become illegal. Never before or since in New Jersey politics has a single issue so divided the voters.

On the wet side of the issue was the Democrat, a Jersey City politician with the mellifluous name Edward I. Edwards. His Republican opponent was a party stalwart from Trenton with the unforgettable moniker Newton A. K. Bugbee.

During the six-week contest, Edwards and Bugbee traveled furiously by train and auto from town to town, shouting out their promises and deriding their opposition to the accompaniment of brass bands and cheering crowds. Those crowds were mostly male; this was the last New Jersey gubernatorial election in which women were barred from voting.

From the beginning of the campaign, Edwards attacked Prohibition as an un-American assault on personal liberty, and he vowed to veto any state legislation passed to enforce it. He reminded voters that he had been one of the only members of the New Jersey Senate to vote against the Prohibition amendment. The most memorable sound bite to come out of the campaign was Edwards's boast: "I am from Hudson County and I am as

Governor Edward I. Edwards
The key issue in the 1919 gubernatorial race was Prohibition; the winner of
the election was Edwards, who proclaimed, "I am from Hudson County
and I am as wet as the Atlantic Ocean." Special Collections and University
Archives, Rutgers University Libraries—New Jersey Portraits Collection.

wet as the Atlantic Ocean." (A newspaper sarcastically referred to
Edwards as "the admirer of the Atlantic Ocean.") In Trenton he said, "I
am against Prohibition and I am just as wet here in Mercer as I am in my
own county." In Metuchen he said: "I will tell you plainly, that if elected,
I am going to do everything legally possible to prevent the enforcement
of the Prohibition law in New Jersey."

The Republicans at first hoped the issue would go away. Bugbee
argued that Prohibition was now the law of the land, and it was useless to
debate it. But when Edwards continued to beat the anti-Prohibition
drum, Bugbee struck back. The Republican candidate charged that if his
opponent were to be elected, "it would mean that the majority of the people of New Jersey desire the nullification of the Constitution, the rock
upon which our Government has been built into a citadel of strength that
has made us the foremost among the nations of the world." Borrowing

language from the Russian Revolution and the American Civil War, he labeled Edwards a Bolshevik and a secessionist. In Gloucester County, Bugbee blasted the "doctrine of treason and anarchy that is being preached by the Democratic candidate," and he accused his opponent of appealing to the worst prejudices of the voters. He said the issue was "law and order against lawlessness; patriotism against sedition."

The same abstract theme was sounded in Republican newspaper advertisements. A typical ad said of Edwards: "Either he proposes to put New Jersey outside the pale of the United States, making it secede from the Union and renounce the Constitution and the Flag, or else he is just a political buccaneer and mountebank seeking to extract votes from New Jersey's intelligent electorate under false pretenses." Asked the ad, "Do You Want New Jersey to Be an Outlaw among States?"

The Republicans believed they had the vote of the "solid, self-respecting people of New Jersey" behind their candidate. Bugbee was endorsed by the Anti-Saloon League and the State Conference of Ministers.

But while the forces of morality may have been rallying to Bugbee, there was evidence that his message about constitutional principles was not reaching everyone. When he appeared at a sewing-machine factory in Elizabeth, a worker in the audience shouted, "To hell with him! He is the man who would take away our beer."

The Republican Bugbee and the Democrat Edwards were actually much alike. Both were moderates, who had won in the primary against extremists on the Prohibition issue. Both were devout churchgoers, both had successful careers in the banking industry, and both had served as state comptroller. There was one ironic difference. The wet Edwards was actually a teetotaler; the dry Bugbee was a social drinker who occasionally had a beer. The voters were amused by the fact that a Republican wet dry was running against a Democratic dry wet.

There were, of course, other issues in the air that autumn of 1919. Around the nation, terrorist bombs set off by radicals and widespread industrial strikes were generating fear of communist subversion. A proposed amendment to give women the right to vote was moving slowly through the states. In Washington, the Senate was bitterly debating whether the United States should join the League of Nations. In New Jersey, there was opposition to an increase in trolley fares from a nickel to seven cents. Edwards accused Bugbee of being a tool of the hated trolley monopoly; Bugbee fired back that his opponent was a tool of Jersey City mayor Frank Hague, a hated political boss.

But the Red Scare, women's suffrage, the League of Nations, trolley fares, and bossism mattered little in the mind of New Jersey voters before the overwhelming issue of whether or not a person would be able to get a drink. A week before the election, the Volstead Act enforcing Prohibition was passed by the Republican U.S. Congress over the veto of Democratic President Woodrow Wilson. Newspapers around the state were suddenly filled with reports of saloons and breweries preparing to close down.

On the eve of the election, many observers thought that Bugbee still held the edge. Republicans calculated that Bugbee could carry seventeen of the state's twenty-one counties and win by thirty-five thousand votes. There was heavy betting on the outcome: the *Trenton Evening Times* reported that the odds were six to five in favor of Bugbee. The members of a Republican club in Trenton reportedly bet $15,000 on their candidate.

The Republicans should have kept their money in their pockets. Edwards won by the respectable margin of fourteen thousand votes. Immigrant groups that had previously voted Republican, notably the Germans and Italians, went in large numbers for Edwards. The Democrat also took cities like Newark, Jersey City, Trenton, and Elizabeth, offsetting Republican majorities in rural parts of the state. In a personal humiliation, Bugbee even lost his home district, Trenton's Second Ward, to Edwards.

As governor, Edwards did just what he promised by opposing attempts to enforce the Volstead Act. During his term, New Jersey indeed became one of the wettest states in the nation.

The historian Warren E. Stickle says the Applejack Campaign heralded profound changes in American politics. The shift of city dwellers and immigrant groups to the Democratic Party as a result of the Prohibition issue marked the beginning of a national political realignment that would put Franklin D. Roosevelt in the White House fourteen years later.

31   Swan Song for Shoeless Joe

It was great ball-game weather in New Jersey on Sunday, June 25, 1922. The sky was clear, with afternoon temperatures in the seventies and a cooling breeze from the southwest. In Hackensack, two thousand eager fans packed a local field known as the Oval to watch the hometown semi-pro team take on a visiting club from Westwood.

But the game did not go well for Hackensack. The Westwood team had a new center fielder, listed in the roster as Josephs, who put in a solid performance. Besides hitting a single and a double, he smacked a home run over the fence. His fielding was just as awesome—he caught a hit to the outfield and rifled it to home plate in time to get out a runner from second base. Thanks to the lanky player, the Westwood team won the game, 9 to 7.

The Hackensack players smelled something fishy. They heard the members of the visiting team call their center fielder "Jackson." And there was something familiar about the man's unique batting stance. The Westwood captain finally admitted the truth. "Josephs" was actually Joseph "Shoeless Joe" Jackson, the former star player for the Chicago White Sox.

How did the great Shoeless Joe wind up playing two-bit ball under an assumed name on a Jersey field? Therein hangs a tale sadly appropriate to the current steroid scandal in baseball.

Joe Jackson was an illiterate boy from the mountains of South Carolina who got his start in baseball playing for a cotton-mill team. His talent propelled him into the minor leagues and then into the majors. At one game early in his career, he played in his stocking feet because he had blisters from breaking in a new pair of cleats. A reporter made up the nickname Shoeless, which seemed to fit Jackson's country-boy manner.

Jackson was popular with the fans, but he would sometimes get teased as a hick, with taunts like "Hey Joe, can you spell 'cat'?" or "Read any good books lately?" Fans who met him on the street would jokingly look down to see if he was really wearing shoes. But the country boy could sure play baseball. In his first full season in the majors, using a homemade bat he called "Black Betsey," he achieved a .408 batting average; his career average was .356, the third highest in baseball history.

Then came his downfall. In the World Series of 1919, seven members of the American League champion White Sox decided they could pick up some serious money from gamblers by deliberately losing to their opponents, the National League champion Cincinnati Reds. The conspirators figured they would need their teammate Jackson, and they approached him with the promise of $20,000. He agreed, and Chicago duly lost the series. Jackson was cheated by the gamblers and by his fellow players, however. He got only $5,000.

Rumors of a fix were widespread, and one of the players, pitcher Eddie Cicotte, finally confessed to Chicago lawmen, naming Jackson and the others who were involved. A nervous Shoeless Joe appeared before a grand jury to tell what he knew. There is a story that when Joe emerged from the Chicago courthouse after testifying that he had taken the gamblers' money, he was met by a group of boys. One of them stepped forward from the crowd and looked up at his hero mournfully. "Say it ain't so, Joe." The baseball star choked back the tears. "Yes, kid, I'm afraid it is." There probably was no such conversation; it seems to have been made up by a newspaper columnist looking for a dramatic story. But the encounter might as well have happened. Jackson and the seven other conspirators, known as the Black Sox, were banned from professional baseball for life by the commissioner, Judge Kenesaw Mountain Landis. (Landis's unusual name, incidentally, came from a Civil War battle in which his father fought.)

Thus it was that Jackson wound up in New Jersey playing outlaw baseball. But his career in the Garden State did not last long. The Hackensack club refused to play against any team that carried Jackson on the roster, and he was dropped by Westwood. A New York promoter tried to put together a team with Jackson and the other Black Sox, but it came to nothing. Shoeless Joe returned south to live out the rest of his life.

There is a legend that he lived in poverty and shame, but it isn't so. The folks back home in South Carolina were more tolerant than those

Yankees, so Joe was able to play a little baseball and coach some local teams. He was married to a local girl named Kitty, and they seem to have had a loving relationship. (She cried when he accepted the gambler's money back in '19.) He opened a Greenville, South Carolina, store and earned a reasonable income: "Joe Jackson Liquor—Joe Jackson, Sole Owner," read his business card. He died of a heart attack in 1951, thirty years after his disgrace.

Many of his neighbors in Greenville thought Joe got a bum deal, and over the years others have joined in that opinion. The South Carolina legislature has passed resolutions calling for his reinstatement in baseball and admission to the Hall of Fame. Books and articles have been written in his defense, and there is a Joe Jackson Society in South Carolina that lobbies on his behalf. Jackson is portrayed as a romantic innocent in the movie *Field of Dreams*.

Jackson's defenders cite many facts. They point out that Jackson was never found guilty—he and the other Black Sox were acquitted by a Chicago jury. Jackson himself said that he was never part of the inner circle of players who met with the gamblers. Besides, he said, he played the Series as best he could. And, in fact, during the Series he achieved the highest batting average and the most hits of any player on either team. A scholarly article in the November 1993 issue of *The American Statistician*, using sophisticated mathematical techniques like regression analysis, claims that Jackson played to win.

Jackson's supporters say that if there was a fix, the owner of the Chicago White Sox, Charles Comiskey, deserves a share of the blame. They paint Comiskey as a cheapskate who, even by the standards of the day, underpaid his players and treated them shabbily, so that in desperation they turned to an alliance with gamblers. One famous Comiskey story is that he promised a pitcher a bonus if he won thirty games, and then benched him after he won twenty-eight. (What would those old players think of our age of multimillion-dollar salaries, free agents, and a powerful players' labor union?)

Unable to read or write and innocent of the legal danger he faced, say his supporters, Jackson was coerced by Comiskey into testifying before the grand jury without having his own lawyer. But let us not get carried away by our sympathy. Joe Jackson may have been a nice guy and a simple country boy, but by his own admission to the grand jury, he accepted money from gamblers to take a dive.

In our permissive age, there is something noble about the fact that baseball insists that its players perform honestly, and that a man who violated that rule is barred from the Hall of Fame.

32 The Tragic Fall
of the Mexican Lindbergh

On a July Friday in 1928, an auto mechanic with the appropriate name of John Carr knocked off work early from the garage where he worked in the little Burlington County village of Chatsworth. He picked up his wife and mother in his family car, and drove out eight miles or so from the village to an isolated clearing beside the railroad tracks where local people knew the huckleberries were ready for picking.

The three were all alone in the heart of the vast Pine Barrens. As they began picking berries they noticed something odd: the trees overhead seemed to have been smashed, as if by a giant hand. Curiously, cautiously, they ventured into the woods, following the direction of the splintered trees.

It was hard to see anything in the dimly lit woods. John Carr was ahead of the others when he suddenly came across the wreckage of an airplane in the underbrush. Nearby, he discovered the body of a man lying face down on the ground. The dead man was wearing a leather flying jacket and slippers.

The family drove hurriedly to Willis J. Buzby's general store in Chatsworth, where Carr phoned the Burlington County chief of detectives, Ellis Parker, in the county courthouse at Mount Holly. (For more about Parker, see chapter thirty-five.) Parker directed Detective Arthur Carabine and the acting coroner, John Throckmorton, to drive the twenty-five miles to Chatsworth, where they picked up Carr and headed through the twisty back roads to the wooded crash site.

Carabine and Throckmorton inspected the body. The bones were crushed; clutched in the corpse's right hand was a flashlight. In his pockets they found $175 in cash, a letter in Spanish on the stationery of the Waldorf-Astoria Hotel in New York, and a telegram from the Weather Bureau in Washington. The address on the telegram confirmed what Detective Carabine suspected the moment he saw the corpse: the man at his feet was none other than the famous Captain Emilio Carranza, known as the Mexican Lindbergh.

This was an age when flight was still an adventure, far different from the dreary world of crowded airports and bankrupt airlines. Charles A. Lindbergh was the exemplar of this era, the golden-haired youth who had flown alone across the Atlantic.

Six months after his breathtaking flight to Paris, he accepted an invitation from President Plutarco Elias Calles of Mexico to visit that country. The invitation was prompted by the U.S. ambassador to Mexico, Dwight Morrow, who saw this good-will trip as a way to improve relations between the two countries. Lindbergh may have had his own relations to improve: he had fallen in love with Morrow's twenty-one-year-old daughter, Anne.

Lindbergh made his twenty-one-hundred-mile, twenty-seven-hour nonstop flight from Washington to Mexico City in the *Spirit of Saint Louis*. His visit was an enormous success, and he was saluted by enthusiastic, cheering crowds.

The people of Mexico wanted to return the favor, to show that Mexico could be part of this new world of pioneer aviation, and could produce a hero to match Lindbergh. The obvious choice was Mexico's most famous airman, Emilio Carranza, a twenty-two-year-old captain in the Mexican air corps, accomplished pilot, and the nephew of a former president. A public subscription was taken up to purchase a worthy airplane—a Ryan monoplane, the same type as the *Spirit of Saint Louis*. The craft was baptized *Excelsior*.

On June 11, 1928, Carranza took off from Mexico City to attempt a nonstop flight to Washington. His plane was forced down by fog in North Carolina, but he was still welcomed as a hero when he arrived in the nation's capital. He had lunch with President Calvin Coolidge and was feted by dignitaries.

In New York he was greeted by Mayor Jimmy Walker on the steps of City Hall and set off for another round of festive speeches and dinners. His visit made national headlines, especially when he and Lindbergh flew their planes side by side in a friendly trip to the Midwest. Americans found Carranza, with his youth and modesty, much like their hero Lindbergh.

After a month as a celebrity in the United States, the time came for Carranza to return to Mexico. The manager of Roosevelt Field on Long Island advised Carranza against taking off in the rain with a plane weighted down by an enormous load of gasoline, but the aviator refused to wait. "I pleaded with him not to go," the manager said later.

Carranza took off at 7:05 P.M. on July 12, hoping to make a nonstop flight to Mexico City. It would be the second longest flight up to that time, exceeded only by Lindbergh's flight to Paris. Over New Jersey, Carranza encountered a violent thunderstorm and strayed from his flight path. There was some speculation later that his plane was brought down by a bolt of lightning. But experts who examined the wreckage said that the instruments had been set as if the pilot had been attempting to land.

Lost over the dark Pine Barrens, Carranza was probably using his flashlight to read a map, to check his compass, or even to search the ground for a clearing, when his plane suddenly smashed into the trees. He was thrown from the plane and (one hopes) died instantly. He had been dead about eighteen hours when his body was found by the berry pickers.

The body was placed in a coffin draped with the American flag and guarded by the members of the Mount Holly American Legion Post and a detachment of soldiers from Fort Dix. In New York, ten thousand American soldiers and sailors marched with the hearse taking the coffin to the train station for the trip to Mexico. A nationwide memorial service was broadcast on the radio, and a message of condolence was sent from President Coolidge to President Calles.

In Mexico, where a few days earlier people had been joyously waiting for the triumphant return of the brave aviator, there was weeping in the streets when news of the crash broke. "With all my heart I lament the tragedy of Captain Emilio Carranza," President Calles said. Much attention was given to Carranza's young, pregnant widow, Maria Louisa. They had been married four months. Carranza was buried as a national hero and was the subject of a Mexican folk song, "Ballad of the Murder of Emilio Carranza."

There was oratory in both nations about how the tragedy had brought the United States and Mexico closer together. New Jerseyans took some pride in their role. The Mexican ambassador came to Chatsworth to present a check for $500 to John Carr and $250 to Detective Carabine. New Jersey papers pointed out that none of the local people had taken souvenirs from the wreckage. Later a monument was erected on the site, paid for by contributions from Mexican schoolchildren. Every July, on the anniversary of the crash, a memorial service takes place there, with representatives from the Mexican government and the U.S. armed forces. The Mexican and American national anthems are sung.

Not long ago, the Carranza site was included in a guidebook to "fun," "loony," and "oddball" tourist spots around the nation, which demonstrates that what was an international tragedy in 1928 is only a curiosity to people decades later.

33 On the Boardwalk with Al Capone

Everybody goes to Atlantic City for a convention: teachers, plumbers, salespeople, and (until the departure of the Miss America pageant) beauty queens. So why not gangsters? Back in 1929, America's leading bootleggers, hit men, and racketeers gathered in the city of saltwater taffy to do what conventioneers love to do: talk shop, cut a few deals, and have a good time.

The crime lords came from the nation's major cities. Al Capone himself was there along with other luminaries of the Chicago underworld like Frank Nitty and Jake "Greasy Thumb" Guzik. From New York came a large delegation that included Charles "Lucky" Luciano, Dutch Schultz, Joe Adonis, Albert Anastasia, Meyer Lansky, and Louis Lepke. Among the others in attendance were Charles "King" Solomon of Boston, Abe Bernstein of Detroit, Johnny Lazia of Kansas City, and Waxey Gordon of Philadelphia. New Jersey was represented by Abner "Longie" Zwillman and the host, Enoch "Nucky" Johnson of Atlantic City.

The problem the mobsters faced was that competition was getting out of hand. Rival gangs were muscling in on one another's territory. Only a few months before, seven Chicago gangsters had been gunned down in the St. Valentine's Day Massacre by the Capone gang.

So for the first time, gangsters from all the ethnic groups met to talk things over. It is not clear whose idea it was: some historians of crime think it was Frank Costello; others say Johnny Torrio or Lansky or Luciano, or even Capone. Most likely it was one of those ideas whose time had come. Atlantic City was a convenient location for other reasons besides sea breezes: the host, Johnson, controlled both crime and politics in Atlantic County.

The gathering was not particularly secret. Newspapers carried stories about it. This was the era of Prohibition, when Americans cheerfully broke the law by drinking, and the gangsters who furnished the bootleg liquor were celebrities like prizefighters and movie stars. The Atlantic City police said they would arrest Capone on sight, but since at the moment he was not wanted on any charge, Scarface Al (known as Snorky to his uneasy friends) strolled around town unmolested.

One account of the event says that meetings were held in a conference room at the President Hotel; another says the meetings were shifted from hotel to hotel. Luciano said years later that Johnson had originally booked the conference in an exclusive upper-crust hotel, giving the gangsters Anglo-Saxon aliases when he made the room reservations. Luciano said that when the gangsters with the phony names arrived, the hotel manager threw them out, and that Nucky had to hastily move the meeting to the President. Luciano also said that to discuss important negotiations in private, the mobsters would be wheeled in rolling chairs to a secluded beach at the end of the boardwalk, where they would take off their shoes and socks and wade into the water to talk business.

Luciano's account seems unlikely. It is hard to imagine Capone and his peers standing around like storks in the surf. It is also improbable that Johnson, the boss of Atlantic City, would make the mistake of picking the wrong hotel. Capone himself later gave an account to a lawman of what happened at the conference (he was under arrest at the time): "We talked over our troubles for three days. We all agreed at the end of that time to sign on the dotted line to bury the past and forget warfare in the future for the general good of all concerned." The gangsters pledged to respect one another's territory, to work together to bribe the authorities, and to negotiate disputes peacefully. Whether they actually signed a paper to that effect is, once again, doubtful. One other important piece of business negotiated at the meeting was to set up a telegraph service that would flash racing results to illegal betting parlors around the country. One crime writer said that the conference "galvanized the gangs of America into a powerful single unit." That's probably an exaggeration, but the gathering clearly did increase cooperation in the underworld.

What did they do for relaxation? The traditional story is that they spent their evenings as mobsters are supposed to, furiously gambling, drinking, and womanizing. Maybe so, but isn't it possible that they once in a while acted like ordinary tourists, doing things like walking the boardwalk and buying saltwater taffy? That's at least how Capone seems to have behaved. An Atlantic City newspaper described the Chicago gangster: "Seated in a rolling chair at Kentucky Avenue and the Boardwalk yesterday afternoon, puffing on a big black cigar and surrounded by half a dozen henchmen, 'Al' took in the sights of the famous street and breathed deeply and freely of the ozone with apparently no care in the world." Lansky took his bride, Anna Citron of Hoboken, to the convention, and no doubt the newlyweds spent a romantic moment or two on the boardwalk watching the surf roll in.

After it was all over, the conventioneers made their way back to their home territories. Everyone, that is, except Capone. It seems he was driven to Philadelphia to catch the Broadway Limited train back to Chicago. He had some time to kill, so he and his bodyguard, Frank Rio, went to the movies. On the way out of the theater, he was arrested by a Philadelphia police detective who found that the gangster had a .38-caliber revolver in his pocket. (A .38 seems a bit quaint in this day of assault rifles and automatics.) Capone was sentenced to a year in prison for carrying a concealed weapon.

Luciano, as usual, embellished the story. He said that the arrest was planned; that the other mobsters at Atlantic City demanded Capone do some time in jail to take the heat off everyone else. A more likely interpretation is that Capone set up the arrest on his own initiative. He evidently wanted to stay away from Chicago for a while since his arch enemy George "Bugs" Moran, who wasn't invited to the convention, was trying to assassinate him in revenge for the St. Valentine's Day affair. One possible bit of proof is that the Philadelphia detective who arrested Capone was reputed to have known him socially in Florida.

Capone probably expected to spend ninety days or so—the standard sentence for carrying a gun in the City of Brotherly Love— in a suburban Pennsylvania jail. But the uncooperative judge put him away for a year.

Capone's career went downhill after that. Not long after his return to Chicago, he was put on trial for income-tax evasion and wound up working in the laundry at Alcatraz. He died of syphilis in 1947. Many of the other participants in the Atlantic City conference came to a bad end: Zwillman and Nitti committed suicide; Shultz and Anastasia were murdered; Luciano and Adonis were deported; Lepke died in the electric chair; and Johnson went to prison for a decade.

Maybe they all looked back at that pleasant week in Atlantic City as a golden time in their lives.

34 The *Morro Castle* Mystery

It was a bit after 2:00 A.M. on the night of September 7–8, 1934, as the luxury cruise ship *Morro Castle* beat its way up the Atlantic off the New Jersey coast. Outside a fierce nor'easter was lashing the sea with wind and rain. But it was cozy inside the ship. In the main lounge on B deck, a few passengers were still up, and a steward, Daniel Campbell, was serving drinks. One of the passengers took Campbell aside and quietly, so as not to alarm the others, told him that he smelled some smoke.

Campbell went to look for the source of the smell. He found it in the nearby writing room, where he could see smoke pouring out of a locker built into the bulkhead. When he opened the locker, flames leaped out at him.

So began the death of the *Morro Castle.*

The Ward Line's *Morro Castle* was an ultramodern passenger vessel that plied the profitable route between New York and Cuba. In that era, Havana was a slightly naughty holiday spot, and the trip was popular with couples, singles, and business people. This particular voyage from Havana back to New York was uneventful for the 548 passengers and crew, until, after two days at sea, Captain Robert R. Wilmott began to complain that he was feeling ill. When First Officer William Warms went to check on the captain, he found him dead on the floor of his cabin. After years of service, Warms was suddenly in charge of a ship of his own.

But any satisfaction Warms may have felt was short-lived. Less than eight hours after he found the captain, he was informed that his ship was on fire. The blaze spread quickly from the writing room to the rest of the ship. Passengers were shocked from sleep by the choking, dense smoke and raced in panic around the dark ship. Some died horrible deaths trying to escape by squeezing through portholes. Hundreds leaped into the chilly water, and there are tragic accounts of survivors who saw a husband or wife drown next to them. Bodies washed ashore at Sea Girt, Manasquan,

Belmar, and other Jersey resort towns. Steamships in the area and fishing boats from Jersey shore towns picked up survivors from the sea, but in the end 137 crewmen and passengers perished.

Then occurred a bizarre sequel. The smoldering hulk of the *Morro Castle* was being towed north when the cables broke and she drifted free, coming to rest on a sandbar a couple of hundred yards off the beach at Asbury Park, right next to the convention center. The enterprising city manager of Asbury Park made arrangements so that, for a fee, the curious could board the ship to gawk at the damage. Not until weeks later was the *Morro Castle* removed to be broken up for scrap.

The next act of the tragedy was taken up with the official investigations. Witnesses testified that the crew was inept in trying to fight the fire and had callously abandoned the passengers. The first five lifeboats off the ship carried a total of ninety-two crew members and only six passengers. Chief Engineer Eben S. Abbott was one of the first to abandon ship.

Acting Captain Warms was accused of ineptitude and indecisiveness. Critics said that on the night of the disaster he seemed to be in a daze, and that he delayed permitting the radio operator to send out a distress call until the last possible moment. It was also said he made a grave error in judgment by keeping the ship steaming into the wind at high speed, thereby fanning the flames.

The executives of the Ward Line were accused of operating an unsafe ship and of failing to train the crew to deal with emergencies. Why, for example, where there no fire detectors installed in the public areas of the ship? A federal court found the Ward Line guilty of negligence. Captain Warms and Engineer Abbott were sentenced to prison terms, but their sentences were later overturned by the U.S. Circuit Court of Appeals.

There was one hero, however. The chief radio operator of the *Morro Castle*, George W. Rogers, stuck by his station sending out distress signals even while his radio shack was on fire. He had to wrap a wet towel around his face to keep breathing, and he had to raise his feet off the deck because of the intense heat from below. Rogers was awarded a $200 gold medal from his hometown, Bayonne, New Jersey, for his deed, and he made appearances in theaters as the hero of the *Morro Castle*.

But was Rogers in fact a hero? After his fame abated, he obtained a job as a radio operator on the Bayonne Police Force. One afternoon Rogers delivered a package to his supervisor, Lt. Vincent J. Doyle, and then hurriedly left. The package contained a bomb, and in the explosion Doyle lost three fingers from his hand and suffered a broken thigh.

Evidence linked Rogers to the explosion. A note in the package had been produced on his typewriter. Metal, paint, and cement from his home matched that on the bomb. His motive, the authorities theorized, was to win a promotion by removing Doyle. It was discovered that the grotesquely fat, brooding Rogers had a history of mental problems and had been in trouble for theft, arson, and sexual abuse.

Rogers was convicted of attempted murder and sentenced to the state penitentiary in Trenton for a term of twelve to twenty years. He was released in 1942 because of the war emergency, and he worked in defense plants. But a decade later, Rogers was in trouble once again. He was convicted of bludgeoning to death a father and daughter who lived near his home; the motive was robbery. This time he received a life sentence.

Some people have argued that Rogers was guilty of much more; that he was, in fact, responsible for the *Morro Castle* disaster. Those who believe Rogers was culpable say that he planted an incendiary device in the ship's locker, and that he may have poisoned the captain as well. Why? Perhaps out of a desire to become a hero, perhaps from simple madness.

But there are other possible explanations for the death of the *Morro Castle.* The writing-room locker was located near the ship's main smokestack and may have contained flammable material. A flaw in the smokestack could have allowed heat or a spark to touch off the blaze in the locker. Indeed, the fire may have broken out elsewhere on the ship at the same time as the locker and spread quickly because of the highly flammable wood paneling and layers of paint.

It is unlikely that we will ever know whether Rogers was guilty; he died of a heart attack in prison in 1958.

So let us leave the *Morro Castle* where we began, as the ship makes its way up the Atlantic Coast through a storm. The captain lies dead on his cabin floor, radio operator Rogers rests in his bunk dreaming his dreams, and in the lounge, a passenger detects a curious smell in the air.

35  The Rise and Fall of a Great Detective

There is a classic type of mystery-story detective— Colombo, Jane Marple, and Rumpole are examples—who seems like a hopeless rube but who manages to solve the crime and confound the big shots.

Ellis Parker, the chief detective of Burlington County, was a real-life version. Parker was a big man who a smoked corn-cob pipe and dressed in rumpled clothes. He worked out of a dingy, cluttered office in the county courthouse in Mount Holly. The father of fifteen children, he seemed to know everyone in the county by name.

He began his career as county detective in 1892, when he was nineteen years old. In the half century that followed, he solved crimes ranging from horse theft to manslaughter. Newspapers in New York and Philadelphia loved to write about Parker's exploits; about how this one-man, backwoods Scotland Yard was able to solve the most baffling puzzles. It was said that he investigated 286 murders and obtained convictions in all but ten. He became a celebrity, and he was frequently called upon to solve crimes outside Burlington County.

In one 1921 case, a soldier named Greggor disappeared at Fort Dix; his body was found three months later. Parker interrogated all of the men in Greggor's company, and picked out one as the murderer. Why? Because all of the other soldiers had been unable to remember what they had been doing on the day Greggor disappeared; only the murderer came up with a polished alibi.

It was reported of Parker that on another occasion he was able to solve a crime that happened in California by sitting in his Mount Holly office and going over the facts in his head. He was sometimes accused of skirting the boundaries of the law. It was said that he would round up everyone connected with a case and throw them in jail until he was able to ferret out the culprit.

Then in 1932, a world-shaking crime took place in neighboring Mercer County: the infant son of the hero aviator Charles Lindbergh was kidnapped from his crib. Parker keenly wanted to enter the case, but he was rebuffed by the state police and the FBI. From the sidelines he accused the authorities of incompetence, and he refused to believe that the man convicted of the crime, Bruno Richard Hauptmann, was actually guilty.

Then came his big chance. Harold G. Hoffman, the newly elected governor of New Jersey, also came to doubt the guilt of Hauptmann, and he authorized Parker to investigate. For a time nothing happened. But then, less than two days before Hauptmann was to be placed in the electric chair, Parker dramatically delivered to the authorities one Paul H. Wendel, along with Wendel's twenty-five-page confession that he had been the sole kidnapper of the Lindbergh baby. The confession said that Wendel had taken the infant to a Trenton tenement, where it died accidentally. The middle-aged Wendel was a sleazy character. A Trenton lawyer who had been disbarred for perjury, he had a history of embezzlement and petty crime.

This sudden development caused a sensation, and the execution of Hauptmann was postponed while state and Mercer County lawmen investigated. Attorney General David Wilentz rushed to the Mercer County jail where Wendel was being held. "Gee, but I'm glad to see you," said Wendel when he met Wilentz. He then proceeded to tell the attorney general a bizarre story. A month before, he said, he had been kidnapped outside his fleabag Manhattan hotel by three men who took him at gunpoint to a house in Brooklyn. There he had been kept prisoner for a week in the cellar and tortured until he wrote a confession to the Lindbergh crime. His captors had then driven him to Ellis Parker's house in Mount Holly.

Wendel had known Parker for many years and thought the Burlington County detective would help him. But instead Parker, with the help of his son Ellis Jr., confined Wendel in a bungalow on the grounds of a state mental institution—the New Lisbon Colony for Feeble-Minded Males. There Parker pressured the ex-lawyer to write a longer, more detailed confession. Wendel did so, he said, as a way to escape his nightmare. To prove he had been tortured, Wendel showed bruises on his body to Attorney General Wilentz.

Along with the Mercer County prosecutor and the Mercer County Grand Jury, Wilentz concluded that Wendel was telling the truth about his ordeal; that he had nothing to do with the Lindbergh crime. Three days later than scheduled, Hauptmann was executed.

The district attorney of Brooklyn, with the help of Wendel, pressed to unravel the kidnapping of the ex-lawyer. The three Brooklyn kidnappers—Murray Bleefeld, Harry Weiss, and Martin Schlossman—were located and indicted. They testified that they had been hired by Ellis Parker, and that Ellis's son had actually been present in the house where Wendel was tortured. Bleefeld, Weiss, and Schlossman were ultimately sentenced to twenty-year terms in Sing Sing.

Governor Hoffman refused to extradite Ellis Parker and his son to Brooklyn to be tried with the other kidnappers. But Wendel, who was obsessed with the desire for revenge, brought the matter before the U.S. attorney general. A federal grand jury in Newark indicted the Parkers. Ironically, the charge was that they had violated the Lindbergh law, passed in the aftermath of the crime, which made kidnapping a federal offense.

The trial lasted from April 27 to June 24, 1937, the longest up to that time in New Jersey history. It was clear that Parker was guilty—among other things the great detective had been clumsy enough to make traceable long-distance telephone calls from Mount Holly to Brooklyn. Parker was sentenced to six years, and his son to three years, in a federal penitentiary.

Why had Parker done it? The speculation was that he had convinced himself—perhaps with the prodding of Governor Hoffman—that if he solved the Crime of the Century he would be appointed to head up law enforcement in New Jersey. And just maybe this triumph in the Lindbergh case could propel Hoffman to the White House, in which case Parker could replace J. Edgar Hoover as head of the FBI. It may be that Parker actually believed that Wendel had committed the crime.

The Parkers, father and son, lost their appeals, and in June 1939 started their terms in the federal prison in Lewisburg, Pennsylvania. Parker's Burlington County friends tried to get him pardoned, and eight thousand county residents signed a petition for his release. But Parker became ill with what was diagnosed as a brain tumor. He died in the prison hospital on February 4, 1940, at age sixty-eight, with his sorrowing son at his bedside.

When Ellis Parker was sentenced, the judge said to him, "I have the impression that your life as a law-enforcement officer and your position in the community have given you the feeling that you are above the law, and that is the cause of your making a mockery of the processes of justice in New Jersey." After Parker died, an obituary writer at a New York newspaper said much the same thing in a simpler way: the press had turned Ellis Parker into a legend, and "in time Ellis Parker came to believe the Ellis Parker legend."

36 Mommy Was a Commie

A lot of celebrities got divorced in the 1930s, like Humphrey Bogart, Cary Grant, Joan Crawford, Bette Davis, Clark Gable, and Jean Harlow.

But not all the famous marital breakups occurred in Hollywood. One of the best-known splits of the 1930s took place in an obscure home at 38 Lakewood Terrace in Bloomfield, New Jersey. The household consisted of a wool salesman named Warren Eaton, his wife, Mabel, and their two children, ten-year-old Mabel and five-year-old Warren Jr. (Why doesn't a female child named after her mother get to use a "junior" after her name?)

The case went to trial in January 1936 before Robert Grosman, a master in chancery court, the equivalent of a divorce court judge. In her testimony, wife Mabel claimed that during the ten years of their marriage she had been abused by husband Warren. On one occasion, she said, he had pushed her down in the street. Warren shot back that it was Mabel who had committed the violence. He said that on one occasion she kicked him in the groin, causing it to rupture, then threw talcum powder in his face to blind him, and then jumped on him, ripped off his shirt, and bit him on the arm. Another time, claimed Warren, she kicked him while he was setting up toys under the family tree on Christmas Eve. Charming couple, those Eatons.

But there was more. Warren claimed that Mabel had tried to inflict bizarre beliefs on the family. He said that she was a Communist and an atheist, that she despised religion, and that she refused to allow the children to be raised in his Methodist faith. Warren said that Mabel had brought radical literature into the house, including the "Communist Manifesto" and a leftist songbook, and that she was out four nights a week attending radical lectures. According to Warren, Mabel told him that under Communism, the sexes were equal and children were raised outside of the home: "She said that housework was only foolishness, that a woman should be the same as a man." Questioned sharply by her husband's attorney and by Judge Grosman, Mrs. Eaton admitted at the trial that she studied the works of Karl Marx and did not believe in God.

Judge Grosman decided the case in favor of husband Warren and granted him custody of the children. In his decision, the judge said that Mabel's acts of violence against her husband were attested to by witnesses, while Warren's acts against his wife were mostly unproved. Grosman probably should have let it go at that, but he decided to go one step further. He said he was also ruling against Mabel because of her political beliefs.

"It is common knowledge," intoned the judge in his decision, "that the principles of Communism are the antithesis of those generally held by most Americans." Communists, said Grosman, "scoff at the belief in the Supreme Being, in the brotherhood of man, in the virtue of women, the marriage institution, as well as the personal relation between parent and child." Grosman conceded that Mrs. Eaton had the right to her own opinion, but "she is not privileged to instill into the minds of these young children, against the will of their father, these doctrines which she, herself, has embraced and which are looked upon with abhorrence by the vast majority of people living under the protection of our Lord."

The fact that a mother had been denied custody of her children because of her religious and political opinions, reportedly the first case of its kind in the nation's history, made headlines around the country. Most newspaper comment was critical of the decision, calling it an example of boneheaded New Jersey justice and comparing it to the doctrines of the Nazi regime. Under the headline "Jersey Justice Has the Jitters," the *New York Post* editorialized that Judge Grosman probably looked under his bed every night for bearded Communist bombers. "'Wrong Ideas,' So Kids Taken from Mother" ran the headline in an Oklahoma paper. The Communist *Daily Worker* cited the case as proof of creeping fascism.

But some voices in the press disagreed. The *New York Journal* and the *Newark Call* argued that the decision was best for the Eaton children, who would now be allowed to grow up as Americans. A Brooklyn man wrote to his newspaper: "I submit that a woman of Communist convictions, by serving the Marxist ideology with every meal, can easily create a situation for which divorce is the only remedy."

Mrs. Eaton moved from New Jersey to live with her sister in the Bronx, from where she gave interviews to the newspapers about her campaign to get her children back. "My babies mean more to me than anything else in the world," she cried. "Unless I get them back I have nothing to live for." The tabloids described her as an attractive brunette; there was no description of her husband's looks.

The American Civil Liberties Union offered to handle Mrs. Eaton's legal appeal. But the ACLU found her a difficult, quarrelsome client who was prone to making wild charges—for example, that the transcript of her first trial was a forgery. An ACLU attorney concluded that the strong evidence of her cruelty would doom the appeal, and the organization quietly withdrew. Mrs. Eaton retained a new set of lawyers and pressed her appeal with the New Jersey Supreme Court, then known as the Court of Errors and Appeals. The brief filed by Ms. Eaton was like nothing the court had seen. The document declared melodramatically that "Motherhood has never in all its history before been in such danger, and all womanhood now looks to this honorable court for justice herein."

The brief ridiculed the accusation that Mrs. Eaton was a Communist, pointing out that the term had even been used to describe the president of the United States. (Mabel said her husband had called her "a radical red nut like Roosevelt.") And besides, observed her lawyers, even the Soviet Union had laws upholding marriage and morality.

The husband's lawyer, J. Raymond Tiffany, who had handled the case since it began, argued that Mrs. Eaton was a publicity seeker who had no real interest in the children. He said that she had not visited her son and daughter since the divorce and had not even sent Christmas cards and gifts to them. He reminded the court of Mrs. Eaton's alleged acts of rage against her husband. Tiffany cited Mrs. Eaton's dangerous beliefs: she was an active Communist who would raise her children as enemies of the United States. In those days the field of psychology was regarded with some suspicion; Tiffany charged that Mrs. Eaton had left the children at home to go on "psychological weekends" at which she had been unfaithful to her husband.

On April 30, 1937, the court issued its unanimous decision. The judges ruled emphatically that Ms. Eaton's religious and political beliefs were irrelevant to the case; that it had been wrong for Grosman's lower court to have taken them into consideration in determining custody.

The Jersey court decision was a victory for civil liberty and freedom of speech. But it was not much of a victory for Mrs. Eaton. The judges (all male) denied Mabel Eaton custody of the children because of her record of violence toward her husband.

37 The Martian Invasion

On an October night in 1938, a bunch of actors in a Manhattan radio studio convinced a portion of the American public that an invasion force from Mars had landed in New Jersey.

The central figure in this story is Orson Welles, the celebrated actor, playwright, and director. The twenty-eight-year-old Welles had a program on the CBS radio network entitled *The Mercury Theatre on the Air*. For broadcast on Halloween eve, Welles thought it would be fun to do an adaptation of H. G. Wells's old science fiction novel of a Martian invasion of the Earth, *The War of the Worlds*. (H. G. Wells and Orson Welles were not related, by the way.)

H. G. Wells's 1898 novel was set in Victorian England. Orson Welles and his co-producer, John Houseman, decided to change the setting to 1938 America, and the project was turned over to Howard Koch, the program's scriptwriter.

Koch recalled in later years that he was thinking about this assignment as he was driving back on Monday from a weekend trip to visit his parents in upstate New York. It struck him that he should get a map so that he could work out the locales for the script. He stopped at a gas station and asked the attendant for a map. Since this was a section of Route 9 in New Jersey, he wound up with a map of the Garden State. When he returned to his office, he laid out the map on his desk, closed his eyes, and put his pencil point down on the map. Grovers Mill was the place where his pencil landed. Koch liked the sound of the town's name, which is why Grovers Mill became the Omaha Beach of the Martian invasion.

Radio worked fast in those days, and amazingly, the script was written, the sound effects set, and the show rehearsed in less than a week. At 8:00 P.M. on Sunday, October 30, the show was broadcast live on CBS.

Koch had written a major part of the script in the form of radio news bulletins, as if the events were unfolding in what we would call "real time." Listeners hear a weather report, followed by music supposedly coming from a dance band at a New York hotel. This is interrupted by a bulletin announcing that astronomers have seen curious gas explosions on the planet Mars. A professor "Richard Pierson" (played by Welles) from the Princeton Observatory is then interviewed about the phenomenon by reporter "Carl Phillips." Then comes news that there have been earthquake-like shocks within twenty miles of Princeton.

Philips is dispatched to a farm at Grovers Mill, where a fiery object has crashed to earth. The reporter interviews the farmer and we hear crowd noises and police sirens. The glowing object slowly opens up, and the reporter describes what he sees next:

Good heavens, something's wriggling out of the shadow like a gray snake. Now it's another one, and another. They look like tentacles to me. There, I can see the thing's body. It's large, large as a bear and it glistens like wet leather. But that face, it . . . ladies and gentlemen, it's indescribable. I can hardly force myself to keep looking at it. The eyes are black and gleam like a serpent. The mouth is V-shaped with saliva dripping from its rimless lips that seem to quiver and pulsate. The monster or whatever it is can hardly move. It seems weighed down by . . . possibly gravity or something. The thing's raising up. The crowd falls back now. They've seen plenty. This is the most extraordinary experience. I can't find words . . . I'll pull this microphone with me as I talk. I'll have to stop the description until I can take a new position. Hold on, will you please, I'll be right back in a minute.

Then comes the unearthly sound of a death ray, zapping the crowd. There are screams, the microphone crashes, and, as the script says, "dead silence."

An announcer comes on to say that "due to circumstances beyond our control," the radio station is having problems with the broadcast. Soothing piano music comes on the air. But the action soon resumes. Brigadier General Montgomery Smith of the New Jersey State Militia comes on the air to announce that Mercer and Middlesex Counties are under martial law, that homes are being evacuated, and that soldiers are being rushed to the scene. Listeners quickly learn that the soldiers have been wiped out, and Martians are in control of central Jersey. The secretary of the interior warns that the nation must unite to repel the invasion.

More details of the war in New Jersey quickly follow. Artillery and planes fail to stop the enemy. Another alien ship lands at Basking Ridge. The Martians have crossed the Passaic River in giant machines—they are at the Pulaski Skyway, destroying power stations. They are in the Jersey marshes (what we now call the Meadowlands). A desperate operator is heard: "This is Newark, New Jersey. . . . This is Newark, New Jersey. . . .

Warning! Poisonous black smoke pouring in from Jersey marshes. Reaches South Street. Gas masks useless. Urge population to move into open spaces. . . . Automobiles use Routes 7, 23, 24. . . . Avoid congested areas. Smoke now spreading over Raymond Boulevard." (Throughout the broadcast, thanks to Howard Koch's map, real locations in New Jersey are mentioned, including Morristown, the Watchung Mountains, Plainfield, and Bayonne.)

All of this was done in the fashion of radio broadcasts of the day. The horrible news bulletins are accompanied by statements like, "We take you to the Hotel Martinet in Brooklyn, where Bobby Millette and his orchestra are offering a program of dance music." There follows some syrupy music, which is then interrupted by another scary bulletin.

Now while all of this was going on in the CBS studio, a portion of the American public believed that the news they heard from their radio was true. All over the nation, panicked phone calls asking for information flooded police stations, newspapers, and radio stations. Some listeners ran to churches to pray; some armed themselves; some just got in their cars and fled. One New York movie theater received calls from frantic wives trying to reach their husbands in the audience—which led to the entire theater emptying in fear.

A Rhode Island newspaper reported that "weeping and hysterical women" swamped the paper's switchboard trying to find out if the story was true. College students in North Carolina telephoned their parents to come and get them. In Indianapolis, a woman raced into church screaming, "New York has been destroyed. It's the end of the world. Go home and prepare to die." There were reports of persons injured by falling downstairs in the attempt to escape.

In a little town in Washington State, a power failure seemed to confirm that an attack was going on. A number of people said they actually saw the Martian creatures. A woman in Boston said she could see the fires of burning New York City.

The worst was in New Jersey. Two hundred phone calls were made to the East Orange police, more than one hundred in Maplewood. Highways leading out of Trenton were jammed with cars. In Newark, people fled apartments with wet towels wrapped around their heads to shield them from poison gas.

According to one account, a man in Manasquan, driving in a panic away from town, stopped to telephone his cousin in Freehold. "Are the Martians there?" he asked. His bewildered cousin replied, "No, but the Tuttles are, and we are about to sit down to dinner."

The police in New York contacted CBS while the broadcast was in progress, and forty-two minutes into the show, the network interrupted to announce that it was a dramatization. At the end of the program, Orson Welles came on to say that it was "just the Mercury Theatre's own radio version of dressing up in a sheet and jumping out of the bush and saying 'Boo'!" The famed announcer Walter Winchell began his regular broadcast, which came on the air at 9:00 P.M., by saying "Mr. and Mrs. America, there's no cause for alarm. America has not fallen; I repeat, America has not fallen."

There were so many police, reporters, and photographers at the CBS studio that Welles and the cast had to leave by a back door. It is evident that neither Welles, Houseman, nor Howard Koch ever imagined that their program would cause mass panic.

Nobody knows how many listeners came to believe that there was a real invasion going on—this was not the sort of thing somebody would want to admit the next day. Probably the numbers were in the thousands, not the millions. But while limited in numbers, the panic seems to have occurred around the nation.

Why did some listeners believe such a far-fetched story? It's often been pointed out that this was a scary time. Thanks to Nazi Germany's ruthless expansion in Europe and Imperial Japan's in Asia, the world was heading to the war that would break out in less than a year. News bulletins about the crisis were commonplace. There was much frightened commentary about how, if war did break out, America would be defenseless against bombs dropped from enemy airplanes. The public mind was prepared to be shocked—as if in our own era, a fake television news report was issued about a terrorist attack on the United States.

Howard Koch's fine writing ability also deserves credit, or blame, for the effectiveness of *The War of the Worlds* broadcast. He really did capture the tone of contemporary radio. And the actor who played the role of the radio reporter at Grovers Mill was convincing. To prepare for his role, he listened to the recording from the *Hindenburg* a year and half before to study how the reporter's voice had gone from calm to sheer terror.

And yet, anyone listening to the broadcast from the start should have known the whole thing was untrue. The program began with the announcer saying, "The Columbia Broadcasting System and its affiliated stations present Orson Welles and *The Mercury Theatre on the Air* in *The War of the Worlds* by H. G. Wells." But a lot of people missed that opening. It seems that *The Mercury Theatre on the Air* had a pretty minor share of the national radio audience—generally drawing less than 4 percent of the millions who gathered around their radios on Sunday evenings. The big attraction on Sunday nights, which drew an amazing one-third of the national audience, was *The Edgar Bergen and Charlie McCarthy Show* on NBC, a variety program that featured the ventriloquist Bergen bantering with his guests and his imaginary cast of characters. But several minutes into the show, the comedy routine ended and a singer began to warble "Neapolitan Love Song." Some unknown millions of bored listeners at that point twirled their dials to find something else (we would call it channel surfing), and some unknown portion of those unknown millions landed on the Orson Welles program just at the time that the fake news bulletins were coming in from New Jersey.

What was the aftermath? There was some talk of lawsuits against CBS, but they were settled out of court. Orson Welles benefited tremendously from the publicity. He went on to Hollywood where, three years after his Martian broadcast, he directed his masterpiece, *Citizen Kane*, a movie that is invariably at the top of any list of the greatest movies ever made. And Howard Koch? He also went to Hollywood, where he wrote the script for another cinema classic, *Casablanca*.

Little Grovers Mill got to taste a bit of fame too. There is today a historic marker in the community to commemorate the time when America quaked in terror at what was happening in New Jersey.

38  When New Jersey Was a Nazi Target

The 1938 Martian invasion of New Jersey (see chapter thirty-seven) was fictional, but a little over three years later came a real one. In the five months from mid-January to mid-June 1942, U-boats stalked American ships off the East Coast of the United States, sinking eighty-two vessels and half a million tons of cargo—a disaster more damaging to the Allied war effort than Pearl Harbor.

New Jersey stood at the midpoint of the U-boat attack, and much of the carnage occurred off its coast. On January 25, 1942, German sub *U-130* torpedoed the Norwegian tanker *Varanger,* twenty-eight nautical miles east of Wildwood; the explosion shook windows in Sea Isle City and could be heard in Atlantic City. Among the other ships lost off New Jersey was the tanker *R. P. Resor*; when it was torpedoed in February, the flames were visible from Manasquan. In March residents of Barnegat Bay saw fire and smoke from the sinking tanker *Gulftrade.*

It was the admiral of the German U-boat fleet, Karl Dönitz, who realized that because the United States was new to the war, the Americans would lack the dearly bought savvy of the British in fighting submarines. Immediately after Pearl Harbor, he dispatched U-boats to the East Coast.

Dönitz was quite correct; the United States was completely unprepared for submarine warfare. Unarmed and unprotected cargo ships and tankers sailed alone up and down the East Coast with lights on and radios chattering. They were easy prey for the U-boats that came to the surface at night and waited for a target to sail into view. Once in range, the U-boat would cripple the ship with torpedoes and finish the job with artillery fire.

While this slaughter was going on, American warships mostly stood in port and American airplanes stayed on the ground instead of going on regular patrol. When they did venture out, disaster followed: a U.S. minesweeper going after what it thought was a submarine collided with a freighter off the coast of Florida. Off the coast of Virginia, army planes mistakenly bombed a navy destroyer. The destroyer USS *Jacob Jones* was sunk by a U-boat off New Jersey.

One German sub, *U-123*, commanded by twenty-eight-year-old Captain Reinhard Hardegen, sunk three ships in one destructive night in January, without being counterattacked or molested by the Americans. Hardegen and other U-boatmen later remembered the first months of 1942 as the "second happy time," just like the days of easy kills when the war began.

The lights from shore contributed to that happiness. In coastal resort towns along the East Coast, including Atlantic City and Wildwood, lights blazed without any restrictions. At night, U-boats stationed themselves offshore so that ships passing between them and the brightly lit coast became conveniently outlined targets.

Years after the war, a German submariner described what it was like to observe the enemy coast of Delaware Bay from the deck of a U-boat:

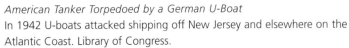

American Tanker Torpedoed by a German U-Boat
In 1942 U-boats attacked shipping off New Jersey and elsewhere on the Atlantic Coast. Library of Congress.

"It was a special experience for us to be that close to the American shore, to be able to see the cars driving on land, to see the lights on the streets, to smell the forests. We were that close."

It took the American authorities a painfully long time to realize that the lights were dangerous, and even then businesses in the resort towns refused to cooperate on the grounds that it would hurt the tourist trade. It was not until March, two months after the sinkings began, that the navy command in Washington issued a timid plea to the East Coast naval authorities: "It is requested that the Commander Eastern Sea Frontier take such steps as may be within his province to control the brilliant illumination of Eastern Seaboard amusement parks and beaches in order that ships passing close to shore be not silhouetted and thereby more easily exposed to submarine attack from seaward." And even then, the results were "dim-outs" rather than complete blackouts. The eminent historian of the U.S. Navy, Admiral Samuel Eliot Morison, described the failure of military authorities and local communities to turn off their lights as one of the most "reprehensible failures" of the American effort in World War II.

Perhaps the only area in which the United States could take pride in those first months of the submarine offensive was in propaganda. The newspapers were filled with entirely false accounts of American counter-attacks on submarines. On one mission an American pilot dropped some bombs where he thought he saw a U-boat. He didn't hit a thing, but the public-relations experts invented a fake quote for him that has been remembered ever since: "Sighted sub, sank same."

Adolf Hitler remarked: "I myself have been surprised at the successes we have met with along the American coast lately. The United States kept up the tall talk and left her coast unguarded."

There were actually very few submarines involved in the attack on America, since Hitler refused to spare Dönitz more U-boats from the European theater. One estimate is that at the height of the East Coast offensive, only a dozen or so were on duty at any one time.

Gradually, the American army and navy authorities learned to fight back. Merchant ships were required to carry weapons, travel in darkened convoys on a zigzag course, and maintain radio silence. American destroyers and planes began to make regular patrols, and private yachts and aircraft were pressed into service. Finally, in mid-April, came the turning point: a German sub was destroyed by exploding depth charges from a U.S. warship off North Carolina—the first U-boat sunk in American waters. More kills followed.

The "second happy time" was ending, and the German command moved the U-boat fleet away from the American coast to the Caribbean and the mid-Atlantic. By mid-June, five months after it had begun, the battle of the East Coast was over.

But in that period, hundreds of merchant seamen died in U-boat attacks. The deaths of those seamen were cruel: some perished in the explosion of the torpedoes; some in the cannonade that followed; some by exposure on the lifeboats; some by the flaming oil that covered the water; many by drowning.

And what of the men who operated the U-boats? Attacking ships at night without warning might be thought of as cowardly, but it was exactly what American submarines were doing at the same time to Japanese shipping in the Pacific. The "second happy time" was the exception; duty on the U-boats was a hazardous occupation and U-boatmen faced death from depth charges and air attack. By the end of the war, over 70 percent of the submarine crewmen had been killed and 87 percent of their U-boats had been destroyed.

They were brave men in a wicked cause.

39 Teleporting Penguin Lands in New Jersey

Charles Fort was a very odd chap. A reclusive, pudgy man with thick glasses and a walrus mustache, he spent his days in musty libraries pouring through old newspapers and books searching for accounts of weird events that seemed to defy the laws of science. Thanks to a family inheritance, he didn't have to worry about working for a living.

Fort (1874–1932) used the stories he culled from library research to write four books: *The Book of the Damned, New Lands, Lo,* and *Wild Talents.* His message was that the stuff we learn in school—gravity, the shape of the solar system, the theory of evolution, and so on—is a bunch of malarkey, and that the scientists who preach it are stuffed shirts.

Fort was a New Yorker, but he drew many of his stories of bizarre occurrences from the Garden State. Indeed, New Jersey gets more space in his collected works than does California, regarded by some as the capital of the weird.

Consider some of the news reports cited by Fort about curious and unexplained events in New Jersey.

On a summer day in 1884, two workers at a farm near Trenton witnessed stones falling from the heavens. In 1929 buckshot rained from the air into an office next to a garage in Newton. In 1902 a shower of mud fell in Jersey towns along the Hudson River. On dates unspecified by Fort, lumps of jelly fell in Newark and Rahway.

A farmer plowing a field near Pemberton in 1859 turned up an axe that was marked with a form of hieroglyphics utterly unknown to science. In 1921 the corpse of a gigantic mammal, similarly unknown to science, washed up on the shore of Cape May. The beast was estimated to be as large as five elephants and to weigh fifteen tons.

In the winter of 1927–28, bullet holes were found in cars and houses in Camden, but no bullets and no sniper were ever found. In 1928 a stranger claiming to come from Mars wandered into a New Jersey town.

And then there was the Jersey Devil, the legendary creature said to haunt the Pine Barrens. Modern scholars treat the J.D. as an example of folk belief. But Fort regarded it as the real thing, and he enthusiastically reported the testimony of Jersey witnesses who claimed to have seen the kangaroo-like beast lurking around farms and swamps.

Fort used these accounts, along with dozens of similar stories from other states and countries, to prove that teleportation (a word he is credited with inventing) takes place all around us. Objects like the stones, the buckshot, the axe, and the Jersey Devil, he argued, were teleported to Earth from a sort of island in the heavens. The jelly was especially significant to Fort; he believed that the Earth was surrounded by a gelatinous layer, and that objects falling to our planet dislodged some of this material.

Spontaneous combustion of human beings and objects was another of Fort's favorite unexplained phenomena. He dwelt at length on a *New York Herald* story of Ms. Lillian Green, the housekeeper of the Lake Denmark Hotel near Dover, New Jersey. On December 23, 1916, the proprietor of the hotel found Ms. Green in her room, dying from burns. The floor under her was charred as were her clothes, but nothing else in the room showed signs of a fire. The woman died without explaining what happened.

In 1927 a barn near Fredon, New Jersey, burned down. The farmer said that for years he had heard strange noises coming from the barn and had seen doors open and shut and pictures sway on the walls, without any human agency at work.

Fort died in 1932, but modern-day Forteans are still keeping an eye on New Jersey. Our state has its own Fortean-influenced magazine, *Weird N.J.* The magazine, which is a fun read for fans of New Jersey, runs stories of ghosts, unusual landmarks, and Fortean curiosities such as the story of an "Indian Curse Road"—a section of Route 55 in Gloucester County, allegedly built over an Indian burial ground. The road crew and engineers are reported to have suffered misery and misfortune. Another article concerns a man who claimed to have been abducted by a UFO just outside the Holland Tunnel.

The 1983 book *Mysterious America* by the Fort disciple Loren Coleman reports on some other cases of teleportation in New Jersey, including a crocodile found in Edison in 1980 and a penguin found in Monmouth Beach 1981. The journal of the International Fortean Organization carried a report about the skeleton of a thirty-foot creature resembling a crocodile that was said to have been found six feet underground at Eatontown, New Jersey, in the mid-nineteenth century. Mixed in with the skeleton, diggers were said to have found a Roman coin.

Skeptics love to poke holes in all of this, arguing that the penguins and the crocodiles reported in New Jersey are most likely abandoned pets rather than teleportees from outer space, that the mysterious beached mammal of Cape May was probably a decomposed whale, and that those Jersey farmers who reported the falling rocks, the burning barn, and the mysterious axe may have been putting one over on big-city reporters.

Consider the case of the hotel housekeeper who seemed to have mysteriously burst into flames. In telling the story, Fort neglected to report a significant paragraph in the *New York Herald* article he used as a source: "County Detective Edward L. Brennan expressed the belief that Miss Green might have been smoking a cigarette which set fire to her night dress. Thomas W. Morphey, proprietor of the hotel, told him that she frequently smoked cigarettes in her room."

As to the shower of mud that hit northern New Jersey in 1902, Fort failed to mention that the original newspaper account quoted a Columbia University professor who said that the phenomenon was probably caused by a rain shower falling through a dust cloud raised by strong wind.

Fort regarded critics like the college professor and the county detective as rationalist killjoys who refused to recognize the mystery and chaos of the universe.

But trying to pick apart Forteanism is probably pointless. Fort himself once said, "I believe nothing of my own that I have ever written," and he refused to join the Fortean Society, established by his followers. A friend of Fort's observed, "He believed not one hair's breadth of any of his amazing 'hypotheses'—as any sensible adult must see from the text itself. He put his theses forward jocularly—as Jehovah must have made the platypus and, perhaps, man." His modern disciples often write with the same tongue-in-cheek quality.

So at its best, Forteanism is sort of a cheerful joke that makes fun of itself, of science, and of the universe in general. It makes our drab world a little livelier and a little more mysterious.

It might be argued that in these days of creeping scientific illiteracy, the last thing we need is skepticism of the scientific method. Maybe the safest approach is to believe in the orthodox explanation of reality—but to keep an eye out for teleporting penguins.

40 The Serpent in the Garden State

A Brief History of Corruption

There is a debate about whether a pervasive culture of corruption exists in New Jersey as compared to other states, or whether we are just better at exposing corruption and rooting it out. There was one person who had no doubt whatsoever about the answer to this question. His name was Lincoln Steffens, and he was one of the muckraking journalists of the Progressive Era, early in the twentieth century. In 1905 his article entitled "New Jersey: A Traitor State" appeared in *McClure's Magazine.*

In this article, Steffens expressed blistering outrage at New Jersey, claiming that what he called "stench of the vice graft" was stronger here than anywhere else in the nation. He condemned the state's citizenry as "mean, narrow, local." To Steffens, New Jersey had been corrupt throughout its history. Steffens was also the man who, after a visit to Lenin's Soviet Union years later, said, "I have seen the future and it works"—truly one of the great bonehead observations of all time. But while he may have been wrong about Russia, was he right about New Jersey?

To answer that question, let me take you on a tour of corruption in the Garden State—a stroll down venality lane, starting in the colonial era and concluding with the twenty-first century. I love New Jersey and wouldn't want to live anywhere else. But there are some aspects of our history that are less than pretty, so forgive me if what follows seems to be a collection of "can you top this" horror stories—a sort of freak show of dishonesty.

At the dawn of the eighteenth century, England decided to bring the contentious colonies of East Jersey and West Jersey together into a single colony under the authority of the Crown. To carry out this mission, in 1703 Queen Anne sent over a distant cousin, Edward Hyde, who bore the title Lord Cornbury, to serve as the first royal governor of the newly united colony.

Alas, Cornbury turned out to be a bad choice for the job. He reportedly accepted bribes from warring factions, set aside great portions of land for his cronies, and persecuted religious minorities. He is also said to have from time to time fannied about dressed up like a woman. A loathing of Cornbury became the one factor that united New Jerseyans, and Cornbury, who the colonists described as a "detestable maggot," was ultimately recalled to England.

That's the traditional view. Patricia Bonomi, a professor at NYU, has argued that Cornbury has been unfairly treated; that the charges against him, from accepting bribes to cross-dressing, were secondhand slanders cooked up by his enemies. Maybe so, but I think that the charges, at least the bribery, have a ring of truth. No subsequent royal governor ever faced such a level of accusations.

The evidence against Cornbury survives in the form of affidavits. One is from Dr. John Johnston, a member of the major group of landholders, who explained how he went to see Cornbury early on in his lordship's term, how he offered a £100 bribe, how Cornbury demurred, saying that he could not accept it, how Johnston left the money anyway, and how he subsequently delivered more. Johnston went on to describe how Cornbury referred to the bribe as a "loan," although neither man ever expected it to be paid back. It all sounds rather like the transcripts of tapes made by a wired FBI informer today.

So in sum, the first known bribe in New Jersey history dates back to the first days in office of the first royal governor in the first years of the eighteenth century.

Now we leap ahead a century or so to the new republic established by the American Revolution and the Constitution. There were great hopes expressed by the Revolutionary generation that the new nation would be a republic of virtue, living up to the noble example of the Roman Republic. One of those with the highest hopes was New Jersey founding father William Paterson.

Ironically, one of Paterson's pet projects as the governor of New Jersey turned out to be an early example of corruption. In 1791 Secretary of the Treasury Alexander Hamilton and his associates formed the Society for the Encouragement of Useful Manufactures, with the goal of establishing a high-tech industrial city in New Jersey, employing the water power of the great falls of the Passaic River. Governor Paterson worked to get the legislature to grant the society a charter, and the city was named in his honor. Tens of thousands of dollars were raised in stock sales, but early on the project nearly foundered on the rocks of human greed. The first director, a speculator named William Duer, had played fast and loose with the accounts of the society, placing the funds into bad investments, awarding himself a $50,000 loan and pocketing $10,000. Duer wound up in debtors' prison.

Equally troubling for those with hopes for the virtuous republic was the persistence of factionalism. A major episode in that new reality was a special election held in Essex County in 1807 to decide whether Newark or Elizabethtown would be the location of a new county courthouse. The town that won the election would become the county seat, which would bring prestige and business. Mass rallies were held on both sides on the eve of the election, and men from Elizabeth were assaulted in Newark. According to accounts of the election, the same voters came back over and over again to cast ballots. The *New Jersey Journal* lamented that "a more wicked and corrupt scene was never exhibited in this State or in the United States." The election was voided by the state legislature.

The scandal at the Society for the Encouragement of Useful Manufactures was really a story of New York speculators, and the Essex County election was at heart a local affair. The truly classic, large-scale sort of corruption involving business and government had to wait for the 1830s, when a new industry arose in New Jersey that required major capitalization, and that actively sought monopoly status and shelter from taxation. We are talking about railroads.

With the development of the steam engine in England and its spread to America, prominent New Jerseyans lobbied for creation of a railroad. Our state, as a transportation corridor between New York and Philadelphia, was the perfect location, and in 1830 the state legislature enthusiastically chartered the Camden & Amboy Railroad. The railroad promised to bring enormous revenue to New Jersey at a minimal cost to its citizens.

In exchange for being granted a monopoly and protection from taxation, the railroad provided stock to the state, with a guarantee that the stock would realize at least $30,000 annually. For many years the railroad lived up to its promise, covering virtually all the state's expenses and making property tax unnecessary.

The railroad's profits were amassed by charging substantially higher rates for passengers and freight traveling through the state than for travel that originated and ended within it. This habit of gouging outsiders has been a feature of other New Jersey tax schemes introduced down to the present day.

But the relationship between the state and the Camden & Amboy turned out to be a Faustian bargain. The corporation's management knew full well that to protect their favored status, they had to exercise control over the legislative process, and in so doing they shaped the political life of the state for decades. Here is how William Sackett, a journalist who chronicled corruption in New Jersey, described the situation. His prose may be purple, but it is accurate.

> Its early alliance with the Legislature of the State, and the popular enthusiasm with which its coming had been hailed, and the State's habit of conceding to it, for the purpose of increasing her own prosperity, whatever privilege or franchise or exemption, or even monopoly, it asked, made it arrogant and aggressive, and it soon came to be recognized as the power behind the throne in the control of all the affairs of the Commonwealth. It went into the counties, picked out its own nominees for places in the Senate and the Assembly, and secured their election to the seats for which they stood. The ambitious politician, hopeful for public honors, had first to make his peace with this rapidly growing monopoly and to secure its favor and consent to his canvass. Such a thing as a candidate announcing his opposition to the railroad company and surviving the election was almost unheard of in State politics. . . . [The railroad] selected the Governors of the State, picked out the men who were to go to Congress, and named the United States Senators. So absolute was its control of all departments of the State government that the State itself came to be known as the State of Camden and Amboy. . . . There never was a more complete master anywhere of the decisions of a state than was this monster monopoly of the affairs of New Jersey. Its enterprise reached out in a thousand different directions, and

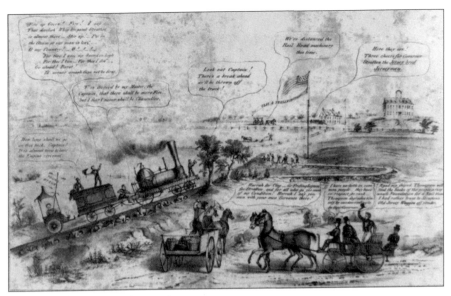

Governor's Race in New Jersey
This 1844 political cartoon shows the debate over the Camden & Amboy Railroad monopoly in the New Jersey gubernatorial election that year. The train chugs along on tracks laid over the people of New Jersey. Library of Congress.

there came a time when the State that had taken the corporation to its bosom as a child began to fear it as a master.

Corruption extended beyond the railroads to other businesses that sought special charters from the state legislature. These charters gave monopoly privileges to the business enterprises that sought them, so were fiercely opposed by rival firms. In one 1855 case, the *Newark Mercury* described as "unparalleled corruption" the report that a state senator had been offered a $700 bribe to vote against a bill to charter the construction of a bridge. In the same year, Assemblyman John Harris of Salem County was abducted from the State House and forcibly put on a train to Philadelphia to ensure that he would not be able to vote on a bill to charter the Mount Holly Bank.

The stage was now set for the great age of corruption that followed the Civil War—the so-called Gilded Age. This was a time when corruption was a national phenomenon, the age of robber barons, urban political machines like "Boss" Tweed's Tammany Hall in New York City, and scandals like the Credit Mobilier affair that involved the Washington, D.C., political elite. You can't blame this all on New Jersey, but you have to admit that our state was an enthusiastic player in the game. There were powerful interests abroad in the state that were willing to buy influence, like the liquor lobby, racetracks, and of course the railroads, which continued to evolve. In 1871 the old Camden & Amboy line was taken over by the Pennsylvania Railroad, and after a ferocious battle in the legislature, the line's monopoly ended and competing railroads were brought into the state. It took another battle to impose taxes on railroad property.

In that era the governorship was firmly in the hands of the Democrats, who elected every state chief executive from 1869 to 1896 and usually held the Assembly. But governors in that era served three-year terms, could not succeed themselves, and had weak veto power. For that reason, real power rested with the so-called "State House Ring," the leader of which was Henry C. Kelsey, who served as N.J. Secretary of State for a quarter of a century.

The State House was not only the scene of corruption, but for much of the late nineteenth century was itself a prime example of that corruption, a sort of palace of plunder. There was an open bar with marble, glass, and mahogany, open for business near the center of the building in the quarters of Barney Ford, the superintendent of the State House and a lieutenant in the State House Ring. By every account, Barney was a popular fellow with legislators, governors, lawyers, judges, and local officials, and reputedly was a go-between in bribery and looting. A friendly saloon with free liquor was part of his hospitality.

The rest of the State House had been spared no expense. It was later found by a Senate investigating committee that the costs of the capitol building had gone from $19,000 in 1888 to $71,000 six years later, that a construction project that should have cost $7,500 wound up costing $27,817, and that a flagpole and flag on the front of the State House cost $1,350. (This was in an era when the average worker made around $700 a year.) Expense accounts were padded with three-dollar lunches—regarded as outrageously extravagant. Printing contracts were enormously inflated. Furniture and carpets purchased for the State House were taken away for private use.

Turbulent Scene in the State House
During the Gilded Age, the New Jersey legislature was the scene of bare-knuckle politics, as seen in this 1887 newspaper image of a battle between Republicans and Democrats for control of the Assembly. Office of Legislative Services Library.

Favorite contractors were making a fortune by overcharging, and the State House Ring was benefiting from kickbacks. The investigating committee was hampered by the destruction of evidence. For example, one State House contractor, Mike Hurley, could not provide records because, he testified, mice had devoured those sections of his ledgers that contained state accounts, leading to a sarcastic reference to "Hurley's discriminating mice." When plans got under way in the 1980s to restore the State House, the architectural researchers were hindered by the fact that very few construction records had survived from the late nineteenth century. They should not have been surprised.

Government in Trenton went from bad to Wertz: specifically George T. Wertz, who was elected governor in 1892. Besides the governorship, the Democrats in that year captured both houses of the legislature. William Sackett, as cynical as ever, observed: "Almost every Democrat who floated to a seat in either House of the Legislature in 1893 represented a ring, or one of the disreputable bosses, or a job, or had been tempted to his candidacy by the hope of illegitimate gain.... Thus everything that was venal or corrupt or offensive in the management of public affairs was largely reflected in the Legislature; and the lawless groundlings who had succeeded in securing their ascendance in State and county and city, found license for fresh excess."

One such excess was to blatantly legalize gambling at the state's racetracks, something public opinion was firmly against but racetrack owners fervently supported. For this action, the Assembly and Senate were derisively described as the Jockey Legislature. Governor Wertz vetoed the bill, but it was passed over his veto. The next election brought in a Republican majority to both houses, but astonishingly, the old Democratic Senate refused to seat the newly elected Republican majority and continued to rule. Governor Wertz went along with this blatantly undemocratic behavior. It was not until the state supreme court ruled against the rump Senate that the legislative anarchy ended. The public was revolted by this behavior. The election that followed brought in a Republican governor, and no Democrat won that post for another fifteen years.

Another hallmark of corruption in this period was an election in Hudson County in 1889 that makes the Elizabethtown election of 1807 look like a church outing.

The poll records indicated that in some precincts the voters had conveniently gone to the polls in perfect alphabetical order, with the Bs following the As and so on. In other precincts the voters had cast their ballots in exactly the order in which they had registered weeks before. Evidently the electorate of Hudson County consisted of anal retentives with a compulsion for order.

The election also featured what were called "joker ballots"—counterfeit, prestamped ballots that were folded inside legitimate ballots so that a faithful party man could cast two or more votes at the same time. The counting mechanism on one box in the Seventh District of Jersey City indicated that 404 ballots had been cast; inside were 507. The counterfeits were crude; one batch misspelled the name Hoboken as "Hoboekn."

And surprise! Many of the voters later tracked down by investigators turned out to be dead. Said Sackett, "Fortunate, indeed, was it for the weak-nerved men and the hysterical women of the county that they knew nothing of a ghostly invasion of the county indicated by the poll-lists till it was all over and the risen cadavers of a past voting era had slunk back in their shrouds to their eternal slumbers again."

It reminds one of former governor Brendan Byrne's remark that when he died he wanted to be buried in Hudson County so he could remain active in politics.

More than sixty Hudson County Democratic officials were found guilty of election fraud. But they served only a few months for their crimes, and the man behind the scandal, Robert "Little Bob" Davis, sheriff and political boss of Hudson County, got off scot-free.

Now all of this may lay corruption at the feet of Democrats, but the GOP in that era was itself cheerfully corrupt. Thanks to the fact that election to the Senate was by county, the more rural, Republican counties were usually able to elect a majority to that branch. The Republican Senate had its own boss in the person of General William J. Sewell of Camden County, described as an "iron-willed Bismarck" of the GOP. Besides being a senator, Sewell was a high-ranking official in the Pennsylvania Railroad and commanded an army of lobbyists and lawyers to protect the line's interests. In this period, Republicans fought to minimize the Irish influence in Hudson County by gerrymandering and establishing commissions to run the major departments of government in Jersey City, a practice called "ripper legislation," which was finally stopped by an amendment to the state constitution.

In sum, the late nineteenth century was a period in which corruption and bare-knuckle politics flourished. But new winds were blowing, and at the dawn of the twentieth century they brought the progressive impulse represented on the national scene by reformers like Teddy Roosevelt.

The ranks of progressives in New Jersey included reformers within both the Republican and Democratic parties. Organizations such as the Women's Christian Temperance Union, the New Jersey Federation of Women's Clubs, and the National Consumer League pushed reforms. Like their brothers and sisters elsewhere in the nation, New Jersey progressives saw as their enemy the old forces of corruption.

The state's progressive movement ultimately came to be personified by one man: Woodrow Wilson, the president of Princeton University, who in 1910 was elected governor of New Jersey on the Democratic ticket. Once in office he pushed through reforms of the election process, workmen's compensation, corrupt practices, public utilities, city government, public education, and labor unions. Wilson defied the state's political bosses and also ended the role of New Jersey as a refuge for monopoly corporations seeking protection from federal antitrust legislation. (It was the latter practice that Lincoln Steffens lambasted in his 1905 *McClure's Magazine* article quoted at the beginning of this chapter.)

It was largely through these reform efforts that Wilson catapulted from the State House in Trenton to the White House in Washington. It appeared to be the triumph of reform; too bad it didn't last.

So far we have witnessed the corruption that bloomed in the state and the nation after the American Revolution and the Civil War. The same occurred after World War I. Certainly, national Prohibition, which went into effect in 1920, was part of the postwar picture. New Jersey was a resolutely wet state. As recounted earlier in this book, one candidate for governor ran on the slogan that he was as "wet as the Atlantic Ocean" and won. As in other urban states, Prohibition was openly flouted in speakeasies.

Prohibition produced an entire generation of gangsters in New Jersey, like Abner "Longie" Zwillman of Newark, who got his start in the crime business as a liquor delivery boy and ultimately became rich from loansharking, crooked unions, bookmaking, and casinos. Bribing government and law-enforcement officials was part of his normal business expenses. Other New Jersey gangsters spawned in this era were Willie Moretti and Joe "Newsboy" Moriarty. It's an interesting reflection of New Jersey's ethnic diversity that Zwillman, Moretti, and Moriarty were, respectively, Jewish, Italian, and Irish.

And speaking of the Irish, this was also the era of Frank "I am the Law" Hague, who served as mayor of Jersey City from 1917 to 1947. Hague was a prime mover in New Jersey political corruption. By controlling the vote in Hudson County, he got to determine who became governor and who those governors appointed to judgeships and commissions. Ironically, Hague first came to power in the guise of a Wilsonian progressive.

Once again, corruption was bipartisan. The worst governor in the period between the World Wars was Harold Hoffman, a Republican, who served from 1935 to 1938. At the time of his death, it came out that he had been on the take throughout his political career. He embezzled hundreds of thousands of dollars from state government operations and from a South Amboy bank for which he served as an officer and was being blackmailed for his crimes.

The pattern of open corruption that followed the Revolutionary War, the Civil War, and World War I does not apply to the post–World War II era. Quite the contrary, the period from the late 1940s to the present has been an era when major reforms were put in place to fight corruption.

In 1947 the state took a significant step forward by adopting a new constitution, creating a modern framework of government, a coordinated judicial system, and a powerful governor. All of this was adopted over the objections of Frank Hague and other bosses who liked the system the way it was.

Measures to prevent corruption followed under the new constitution. A State Commission of Investigation was established in 1968. In 1970 the state adopted sweeping legislation that established the Division of Criminal Justice, making the attorney general the chief law-enforcement officer of the state. This unification of state law enforcement set a national example. In 1973 the Election Law Enforcement Commission was established to monitor the financing of all elections in the state. In the same year, the Executive Commission on Ethical Standards was created. The 1975 "Sunshine Law" opened up meetings of government bodies to the public. The Casino Control Commission was created in 1977. Also in these years, the New Jersey office of the U.S. attorney, aided by the FBI, came to play a much more aggressive role in cracking down on corruption, and regulations were adopted to insure open bidding on government contracts.

The 2001 Open Public Records Act enabled reporters and citizens to obtain government documents, including e-mails that had previously been hidden from view. In 2005 the state began to crack down on "pay to play," the pernicious practice of awarding government contracts to individuals and firms that have contributed to political campaigns.

New Jersey has been fortunate to have a number of governors under the 1947 constitution who encouraged reform, like Alfred Driscoll, who came out of the reform wing of the Republican Party; Richard J. Hughes, who had been an assistant U.S. attorney and later superior-court judge; and Brendan Byrne, who had been Essex County prosecutor, and like Hughes, a judge in the superior court. The U.S. attorneys for New Jersey have on the whole been effective—Frederick Lacey and Herbert Stern in the 1970s stand out. One U.S. attorney, Samuel Alito, who served in that office from 1987 to 1990, is now on the U.S. Supreme Court.

Certainly there have been quibbles about the effectiveness of these measures and these officials, but they clearly represent an attempt on the part of state and federal government to stamp out corruption. Arguably, no other state has established so many agencies and regulations aimed at corruption.

The author is not so stupid as to believe that corruption has been wiped out as a result. We still have corruption and plenty of it, but in my opinion it is being identified and prosecuted more often than in the past. Let's take a look at some of the more newsworthy prosecutions of the period.

Here's one. In exploring the causes of the Newark riots of 1967, a state commission heard allegations of widespread corruption in the administration of Mayor Hugh Addonizio. An investigation led by the U.S. attorney's office found that the city government was indeed corrupt, in fact massively so. It was the old story—to get a city contract, firms had to pay 10 percent of the contract as kickbacks. The city council, the corporation counsel, and the public works department were all involved, with enforcement provided by mobsters from the Boiardo crime family. At the top was Hughie Addonizio himself, who is reported to have told one of the contractors who later turned informant, "There's no money in being a congressman, but you can make a million bucks as mayor of Newark." Another illuminating quote was attributed to Anthony "Tony Boy" Boiardo, speaking to a reluctant contractor, "You pay your 10 percent or I'll break both your legs." Addonizio and his key associates were tried and convicted; Hughie got ten years and a $25,000 fine.

There were other successful prosecutions. I have not been able to find a case of a Jersey government official elected to office while in jail, like James Michael Curley of Boston, but one New Jerseyan came close—in May 1982, state senator and Union City mayor, William Musto, was reelected mayor—a day after being sentenced to prison for taking school-construction kickbacks. This may be the origin of the joke that New Jersey is the place where politicians are investigated, indicted, convicted, and reelected.

Let me provide a bit of personal perspective on this. I spent part of my childhood in Woodbridge, New Jersey. A history nerd even then, I admired the great leaders of American history like Washington and Lincoln and the great documents of government like the Declaration of Independence and the Gettysburg Address. My respect for American government extended to the town mayor, Walter Zirpolo, whom I saw at school and town events. Some years later, I was shocked to read in the newspapers that former mayor Zirpolo had been indicted for accepting an $110,000 bribe to let the Colonial Pipeline Corporation run an oil pipeline and build a tank farm in Woodbridge while he was in office. I think everyone who grows up in New Jersey can recite a similar episode of disillusion. It reminds me of a line from the comedian Lily Tomlin, "No matter how cynical I get I can never keep up."

Another case is that of David Friedland, perhaps New Jersey's most colorful rogue legislator. He was a state senator who faked his own death in a boating accident in order to escape prosecution for a union pension-fund kickback scheme. He was arrested in the Republic of Maldives. While in jail he asked his girlfriend to find a local woman he could marry, hoping thereby to beat extradition. His attempt failed, and he was returned to New Jersey in 1987, where he pleaded guilty to a racketeering charge. Friedland eventually served nine and a half years in federal prison. He was last known to be living in Florida.

The final examples are provided by two governors, three decades apart, who were beset by evidence of corruption in the highest levels of their administrations, and who left office under a cloud—Republican William T. Cahill, who was defeated for reelection in 1973, and James McGreevey, a Democrat who resigned from office in 2004.

I began by asking whether the muckraker Lincoln Steffens was correct when he stated that New Jersey had a deep-seated culture of corruption. The reader is entitled to come to his or her own conclusion on this question, but it is certainly significant that gubernatorial candidates acknowledge that culture, as does a strong majority of the state's citizens in every public-opinion poll that asks about this issue. And there is plenty of evidence of that culture; in January 2005 the *Star-Ledger* published an editorial listing every corruption-related event—such as raids, indictments, and sentencing—in the year just ended, and came up with an average of one every four days.

It is possible to believe, however, that New Jersey has a culture of corruption, without accepting the idea that we are the most corrupt in the nation. A study of public malfeasance was put together by the newsletter *Corporate Crime Reporter* in 2004. Using federal corruption convictions from 1992 to 2003, the study calculated a state-by-state rate per hundred thousand residents. The most corrupt state in the nation, according to this index, was . . . Mississippi (phew!). Matter of fact, New Jersey did not even make the top ten. We came in sixteenth, better than New York, Pennsylvania, and Delaware, to name some neighboring states. The *Corporate Crime Reporter* index is flawed—critics have pointed out that the number of federal convictions may be as much an indicator of the zeal of federal prosecutors as it is of corruption, but it remains the only measure we have.

And we should not take too much comfort in this index. Even if we are sixteenth, that still puts us roughly in the top third of states ranked high on the scale of corruption. So let us inquire into what accounts for the corruption that is here, that might make us more prone than the states at the bottom of the list, like the three with the lowest rate, New Hampshire, Oregon, and, Nebraska.

Two Harvard faculty members, Edward L. Glaeser and Raven E. Saks, crunched the numbers in the *Corporate Crime Reporter* scale with other nationwide data to see what factors about a state seemed to correlate with the corruption rankings. One of the conclusions they reached was that the more ethnic heterogeneity in a state, the greater the level of corruption.

This is certainly the case for New Jersey. Ever since the colonial era, New Jersey has had one of the largest and most diverse immigrant populations in the nation. Today the foreign-born population in New Jersey constitutes about one-fifth of the total. Classically, the traditional ladders to success are closed off to newly arrived immigrant groups, so that illegal avenues become an option. Recall the Prohibition Era trio of Messrs. Zwillman, Moretti, & Moriarty.

Another factor in corruption, it may well be, is the fact that New Jersey has 566 municipalities—more per square mile than any other state in the nation. And we are a home-rule state, where those municipalities have a remarkable degree of authority over zoning and development. An article in the *Star-Ledger* states the problem succinctly: "New Jersey's tradition of home-rule, which places tremendous power in the hands of thousands of local officials, creates a perfect Petri dish for corruption. Land use approvals worth billions of dollars fall to these officials, who often accept campaign contributions from the developers who stand to benefit from their decisions."

So in summary, there are two factors stretching back into our state's history that might help to explain corruption in New Jersey: the diversity of our population and the unshakeable devotion to home rule in our municipalities. The first is a valuable aspect of our society, and the second is a political third rail that will be with us for a long time.

———————

In closing let me summon up a fantasy. I like to imagine that all of those grifters, embezzlers, shakedown artists, and crooked pols from New Jersey history somehow have a place in the afterlife where they can get together after a hard day in purgatory. I imagine a bar, run by Barney Ford like he did in the State House, with liquor provided by Longie Zwillman. I see at the bar Hughie Addonizio of Newark, and Frank Hague, and Harold Hoffman, Walter Zirpolo, and William Duer, all talking shop. You will notice that the company is all male—not surprising since for most of New Jersey history women have been kept out of the back rooms of political power. But here comes Lord Cornbury, who has put on a nice little cocktail dress for the occasion. The group is waiting to greet David Friedland when he passes on, and who knows how many others will follow him later.

The one thing we can be sure of from the history of New Jersey is that there will be others, many others.

POSTSCRIPT

How to Write an Encyclopedia of New Jersey in Nine Easy Years

If reading this book has piqued your interest in the Garden State and you would like to know more, there is another book I would like to recommend—the *Encyclopedia of New Jersey*, which can be found on the shelves of most libraries in the state. It's a pretty hefty tome, weighing in at six and a half pounds, with 926 pages, nearly 3,000 entries, 585 illustrations, and 130 maps, all about New Jersey.

I was part of the group behind that big book, and let me raise the curtain to explain how it came to be. Its origins lie in the widely held attitude on the part of fans of New Jersey that our state lags behind others in appreciating its heritage. A study done in the 1990s showed that among the original thirteen states, New Jersey ranked dead last in the number of history publications written about it, relative to the size of its population. We deserved better. After all, New Jersey was a key player in the American Revolution, as well as in the growth of industry, transportation, science, and technology in the nation created by that Revolution.

So how to tell the story of our state to a wider audience? In 1995 Yale University Press published the *Encyclopedia of New York City*. The work was well reviewed and was a bestseller for the Press. I bought a copy and admired the way it brought together information about the Big Apple from many different perspectives. Browsing the entries that began with "Ch" for example, you would see within the space of a few pages entries on Chinese immigrants, Chock Full O'Nuts coffee, cholera, and choruses—all brought together by the random results of alphabetical order.

I approached Rutgers University Press with the idea of doing something along the same lines for New Jersey. The director, Marlie Wasserman, saw this as an opportunity to advance the Press's contributions to the state and urged me to develop the idea. I naively believed that it would not be very daunting—just identify some topics, get some experts on each of those topics, and have them write. It did not take me long to realize that the project was too enormous for one person to manage. So I approached a friend, Professor Maxine Lurie of Seton Hall University, to join with me as coeditor. She agreed, and ever since, we joke that my asking her was one of the best decisions I ever made, and that accepting was one of the worst she ever made.

One of the first things we did was to make an appointment to see Professor Kenneth Jackson at Columbia University, who had edited the *Encyclopedia of New York City*. Jackson met us with great courtesy in his faculty office and gave thoughtful advice when we asked him what he had learned from his experience. He warned us that we should avoid over-editing the entries; too many layers of editors marking up the copy could stifle the voice of the writer. He also warned us that errors would inevitably creep into the work, and he took down from a shelf a copy of the *Encyclopedia of New York City* with a profusion of yellow Post-it notes sticking out like pastrami from an overstuffed deli sandwich; he explained that each Post-it note represented an error that somebody had found in the text and that Jackson hoped to correct in later editions.

But errors aside, he was immensely proud of the volume, and was convinced that it had contributed to the revival of New York. He was also convinced it was one of his greatest personal accomplishments and predicted that, when he died, his obituary headline would be, "Kenneth Jackson, edited *Encyclopedia of New York City*." (Maxine and I remain curious about what our obituaries will say.)

Jackson told us that it had taken ten years to complete the project. Maxine and I looked at each other in amazement. Surely, we said to each other on the train going back to New Jersey, it would not take us that long. And we were right; it took us only nine years.

Early on we decided not to do just history but to cover contemporary topics too. We agreed with Jackson that a strict A-to-Z format was the best way to organize the work. We decided that we would have to include entries on all governors, municipalities, and counties. But what to include beyond that? We wrote a list of the main areas we wanted to cover, such as architecture, business, literature, science, art, and religion, and we assembled an editorial board of experts from each of these fields. Each expert was asked to come up with a list of a hundred suggested entries in his or her field, along with suggested authors.

To make it possible to start assigning these topics, we started working out the length. We decided that the maximum length would be two thousand words, and this would be reserved for the broadest of categories. Less cosmic entries could be a thousand words, five hundred, three hundred, or one hundred. So for example, the agriculture entry would be two thousand, with shorter entries for specific crops like tomatoes and blueberries.

So far, so good. But as the list of topics kept growing we wrestled with what actually constituted a New Jersey subject. Tomatoes and blueberries were obvious candidates because New Jersey is a major producer of both. Ditto horseshoe crabs, of which New Jersey has the largest population. But what about bears? We decided to include them in the *Encyclopedia* because the encroachment by humans on areas inhabited by bears has become a public-policy issue in our state. We also did an entry on auto theft; at that time New Jersey led the nation in that crime category.

One of the things Ken Jackson cautioned us about was doing entries about prominent living people because their lives inconveniently keep changing after the entry is written. At first we resolved that we had to include living governors, but would stop there. When they heard this, many people argued that we absolutely could not have an encyclopedia of New Jersey without including one of its favorite sons, Frank Sinatra, who was alive when we started the project. Then the argument was that if we had Sinatra, we had to have Bruce Springsteen, so we yielded on that point too. Then came the argument that if we included Bruce, we had to have Jon Bon Jovi, and so it went. (We were sad when Sinatra died, but relieved that his entry would no longer have to be revised.) Jackson was of course quite right about the problem—people you write about can go on to get married, divorced, and indicted.

As the work progressed and entries started coming in, we started a simple database containing the name of the entry and the suggested author. But the list of fields grew exponentially as we realized we had to include the author's address, when we received the entry, where it was in the editing stage (i.e., assigned, completed, returned to author for changes), etc. We hired a graduate student in computer science to expand the database. We also hired his girlfriend to do some of the data entry. We discovered the limitations of using part-time student help when, after the two quarreled and broke up, the grad student stopped coming in to work on the database because he didn't want to encounter his ex.

I have been using the word "we" so far to represent Maxine, Marlie, and me. But the number of people involved in the project kept on increasing. Maxine and I both had day jobs, so were working on the project part-time. Marlie provided room for the project at Rutgers Press on the university's Piscataway campus, and hired a full-time assistant editor. By the end of the project we had hired three—but not all at the same time. The problem with the assistant-editor job was that the better you were at it, the sooner the work would be completed, and the sooner you would be out of a job, so the turnover was understandable. Over the course of the project, there were around a thousand people involved, including 792 authors, plus student workers, Rutgers Press staff members, editorial-board members, an illustrations editor, and a mapmaker.

All of this was expensive, so a major fund-raising effort was undertaken. We were very fortunate that a member of the Rutgers University Foundation, the fund-raising arm of the university, saw the potential of the project and took it under his wing. Through donations, grants, and an appropriation from the state legislature, we raised approximately one million dollars. This fund-raising enabled us to keep the cost of the volume at a reasonable price. Marlie reckoned that $50 was a break point. A person seeking to buy a copy of the *Encyclopedia* to give as a gift would probably balk at anything over fifty dollars. The price that was finally established? $49.95.

And so the project continued, but at a slower pace than anyone expected. I had clearly been overly optimistic about the ease of getting entries. It was often difficult to find experts in a particular field—one assistant professor I asked to write an entry politely declined, saying that he could get tenure by writing encyclopedia entries and a book, or he could get it by just writing a book.

A different sort of problem came from a few authors who submitted what we came to call "ads." Rather than an objective entry on, say, a community college, we would get a puff piece promoting the institution as a world leader in advanced education. In a case such as this, we would have to ask the author to rewrite the entry, or we would have to find somebody else to do the job.

Another category consisted of authors who felt their subject deserved more space than we allowed, arguing that they could not possibly stick with the two-thousand-word limit. And there were those who did not keep the focus of their subject essay on New Jersey but strayed well beyond its borders. One such writer accused me of being like a prison warden who wanted to divide human knowledge into separate entries and place each one in its own locked cell. I have to admit that he was right and had come up with a pretty good metaphor for what encyclopedias do.

We paid authors ten cents a word, which is the standard for reference works but does not encourage authors to put the assignment on the top of their priority list. A lot of time was spent writing dunning letters to authors whose entries were overdue. We also tried a few freelancers who boasted they could research and write about anything. Alas, we found that most could not.

But these bad examples aside, most authors took their work for the *Encyclopedia* seriously and devoted much time for little compensation. Consider, for example, the entry on "dance." It was assigned to a professor in the performing arts program of Rutgers who was herself a former professional dancer. As she sat down to write she discovered that nothing had ever been written on the subject of the history of dance in New Jersey. So she became the first, and in the end produced a fine, informative entry that will serve as the starting point for anybody who wants to write on the subject.

Maxine and I read and edited every entry. If we disagreed, we would have a meeting to iron out our disagreement, keeping in mind Ken Jackson's warning about over-editing. We also looked at every illustration that was submitted to decide whether or not to use it. We usually agreed, although at one time tussled over a photo of Albert Einstein riding a bicycle. It was a great illustration, but we decided not to use it because it was taken when the great scientist was in California, not in Princeton.

It may seem from the above that we did one thing at a time—first coming up with a list of entries, then assigning them to writers, then editing the entries, doing fund-raising, and so on. Not so—everything was happening at the same time. Maxine came to refer to the project as the biggest jigsaw puzzle ever.

Toward the end of the project, I left my day job to take a new position. I continued to work on the *Encyclopedia*, but Maxine stepped in to do a greater share, for which she has my profound thanks.

Marlie did a truly heroic job of pressing us onward to a conclusion, setting deadlines for the work to be finished that we editors routinely blew past. But at last we were able to end the writing stage and turn the project over to the Press production and marketing staff to make it into a real book that people could buy and read. It was finally published in April 2004. I am glad to report that the book was a success, with great reviews and three printings. The New York Public Library named the book one of the top reference works of 2005.

At the beginning of the project we agreed that the goal would be to produce a work that would educate the general public about the state of New Jersey and also provide a starting point for scholars, students, and indeed anybody who wanted to write about New Jersey. I think those goals were met.

Which leads me to think about Samuel Johnson, that great, crabby eighteenth-century English man of letters. He spent nine years (from 1746 to 1755) writing his pioneering *Dictionary of the English Language*, without benefit of computers, libraries, photocopy machines, fund-raisers, press releases, or other modern-day phenomena. When it was published he wrote an introduction in which he compared his work on the dictionary to the story of a primitive tribe who saw the sun rising over a hill. The tribe climbed the hill to reach the sun, only to find it over a more distant hill, just as far away. In the same way, he said, the work on his dictionary had ended, but was not completed. It is a sentiment that those of us who labored on the *Encyclopedia* can understand: the work of describing New Jersey will continue, helped along, we hope, by our climb up the hill.

SUGGESTIONS FOR FURTHER READING

This section is for readers who want to find more information about the subjects covered in this book. I have included books, articles, and Web sites that are readily available, as well as hard-to-find sources, such as out-of-print books and old newspapers. For those obscure sources, readers are advised to visit archival collections such as the Special Collections division of Rutgers University Libraries, the New Jersey State Archives, and the Charles F. Cummings New Jersey Information Center at the Newark Public Library. Readers with questions or comments are also welcome to contact me at my e-mail address, mmappen @gmail.com. And readers who wish to delve deeper into the history of the great state of New Jersey or who have questions are cordially invited to join H-New-Jersey, a computer discussion network that can be found at h-net.org.

INTRODUCTION
Many of the jokes can be found in the entry on "Jersey Jokes" written by Peter Genovese and Marc Mappen and the entry on "Image" written by Michael Rockland in the *Encyclopedia of New Jersey* (New Brunswick: Rutgers University Press, 2004).

1. HOW WE GOT TO WHERE WE ARE
Michael Rockland's essays about New Jersey, including his fine entry on "Image" in the *Encyclopedia of New Jersey*, have informed this chapter. The following two books also delve into enduring characteristics of our state: Alan Karcher, *New Jersey's Multiple Municipal Madness* (New Brunswick: Rutgers University Press, 1998) and Angus Gillespie and Michael Rockland, *Looking for America on the New Jersey Turnpike* (New Brunswick: Rutgers University Press, 1989).

2. WHEN PREHISTORIC ELEPHANTS ROAMED NEW JERSEY
Two publications discuss mammoths and mastodons in the Garden State: *A New Jersey Mastodon*, Bulletin 6 (Trenton: New Jersey State Museum, 1964) and William Gallagher et al., "Quaternary Mammals from the Continental Shelf off New Jersey," *The Mosasaur: The Journal of the Delaware Valley Paleontological Society* 14 (October 1989): 101–110. The definitive book on New Jersey's Native Americans, which also has information on prehistoric animals and on the Lenape stone and the Holly Oak pendant hoaxes, is Herbert Kraft, *The Lenape: Archaeology, History, and Ethnography* (Newark: New Jersey Historical Society, 1986).

3. NEW JERSEY WAS PARADISE

A fine compendium of early travelers' accounts is Miriam V. Studley, *Historic New Jersey Through Visitors' Eyes* (Princeton: D. Van Nostrand Company, 1964). Accounts by the first Dutch settlers can be found in John Franklin Jameson, ed., *Narratives of New Netherland, 1609–1664* (1909; reprint, New York: Barnes & Noble, 1967).

4. MOVE OVER, BETSY ROSS

A discussion of Hopkinson's role is in Earl P. Williams, "The 'Fancy Work' of Francis Hopkinson: Did He Design the Stars and Stripes?" *Prologue: Quarterly of the National Archives* 20 (Spring 1988): 42–52. An informative book that covers the flag's origins is William Rea Furlong and Byron McCandless, *So Proudly We Hail: The History of the United States Flag* (Washington, D.C.: Smithsonian Institution Press, 1981). For Betsy Ross's place in history, see Laurel Thatcher Ulrich, "How Betsy Ross Became Famous: Oral Tradition, Nationalism, and the Invention of History," *Common-Place* 8, no. 1 (October 2007) at www.common-place.org.

5. GOOD GOLLY, MISS MOLLY

The hands-down best book on this subject is David G. Martin, *A Molly Pitcher Sourcebook* (Hightstown, NJ: Longstreet House, 2003).

6. THE CALDWELL MURDER CASE

The pamphlet written by the Reverend Caldwell about the death of his wife is James Caldwell, *Certain Facts Relating to the Tragic Death of Hannah Caldwell, Wife of Rev. James Caldwell* (Elizabeth, NJ: reprinted in 1934). Captain DeHart's critique has been collected in a pamphlet: *The Caldwell Controversy* (Elizabethtown, NJ: Essex Standard, 1846). A biography that brings together information from many sources is Norman F. Brydon, *Reverend James Caldwell, Patriot, 1734–1781* (Caldwell, NJ: Caldwell Centennial Committee, 1976). Thomas Fleming, *The Forgotten Victory: The Battle for New Jersey—1780* (New York: Readers Digest Press, 1973) is a rousing account of the military struggle that drew in James and Hannah Caldwell.

7. "THE COW CHACE"

A well-written book about Major André is James Flexner, *The Traitor and the Spy: Benedict Arnold and John André* (New York: Harcourt, Brace, 1953). Another is John Evangelist Walsh, *The Execution of Major André* (New York: St. Martin's Press, 2001). A book about the Jersey battle that inspired André's poem is Charles H. Winfield, *The Block House at Bull's Ferry* (New York: W. Abbatt, 1904).

8. CLASSICAL GAS

An account of the Millstone River experiment written by Paine himself can be found in *The Life and Writings of Thomas Paine* (New York: Vincent Parke, 1908).

9. THE CONGRESSMAN'S COLD

This episode is discussed in the larger context of Thomas Jefferson's thoughts, in John Chester Miller, *The Wolf by the Ears: Thomas Jefferson and Slavery* (New York: Free Press, 1977). An overview of the Ordinance of 1784 can be found in Robert F. Berkhofer Jr., "Jefferson, the Ordinance of 1784, and the Origins of the American Territorial System," *William & Mary Quarterly* 29 (1972): 231–262.

10. THE FIRST FLIGHT

Two out-of-print pamphlets tell the story of the balloon flight in detail: Alan Drattell and Jeanne O'Neill, *Journey to Deptford* (Deptford, NJ: Township of Deptford, 1976) and Carroll Frey, *The First Air Voyage in America* (Philadelphia: Penn Mutual Life Insurance Company, 1943).

11. JOHN ADAMS'S ASS

A good account of the crackdown on dissent is James Morton Smith, *Freedom's Fetters: The Alien and Sedition Laws and American Civil Liberties* (Ithaca, NY: Cornell University Press, 1966). Smith focuses on the Baldwin case in his article "Sedition, Suppression, and Speech: A Comic Footnote on the Enforcement of the Sedition Law of 1798," *Quarterly Journal of Speech* 40 (1954): 284–287.

12. MAN EATS TOMATO AND LIVES!

The whole story of the tomato hoax is explored in Andrew F. Smith, "The Making of the Legend of Robert Gibbon Johnson and the Tomato," *New Jersey History* 108 (Fall/Winter 1990): 58–73.

13. EXPLOSION ON THE USS *PRINCETON*

A colorful article about the explosion is Donald B. Webster Jr., "The Beauty and Chivalry of the United States Assembled . . . ," *American Heritage* 17 (December 1965): 50–53, 87–90.

14. TWO NEW JERSEY SOLDIERS IN CONFEDERATE PRISONS

Two publications tell the story of these New Jersey prisoners of war. The first is Carlos E. Godfrey, *Sketch of Major Henry Washington Sawyer, First Regiment, Cavalry, New Jersey Volunteers; a Union soldier and prisoner of war in Libby Prison under the sentence of death* (Trenton: MacCrellish & Quigley, 1907). The second is William B. Stypel and John J. Fitzpatrick, eds., *The Andersonville Diary and Memoirs of Charles Hopkins, 1st New Jersey Infantry* (Kearny, NJ: Belle Grove Publishing Co., 1988). The Web site for Andersonville National Park is www.nps.gov/ande/www.nps.gov/ande/.

15. GENERAL GRANT SKIPS THE THEATER

Grant recounted his actions before and after the assassination in his autobiography, *Personal Memoirs of U. S. Grant*, which has been issued in many different editions since its original publication in 1885–86. An acclaimed book about the general's life deals at length with the assassination: William McFeely, *Grant: A Biography* (New York: W. W. Norton, 1981). The Web site for the Ulysses S. Grant National Historic Site is www.nps.gov/ulsg and for Grant's Tomb (a.k.a. the General Grant National Memorial) is www.nps.gov/gegr.

16. THE JERSEY GENERAL AND THE SECRET OF CUSTER'S LAST STAND

Articles and letters by General Godfrey, along with much more material, can be found in W. A. Graham, *The Custer Myth: A Source Book of Custeriana* (Harrisburg, PA: Stackpole, 1953). An excellent biography of Godfrey is William E. Moody, "Soldier of Valor," *Research Review: The Journal of the Little Big Horn Associates* 15 (Winter 2001): 12–30. The Web site of the Little Bighorn Battlefield National Memorial is www.nps.gov/libi.

17. POOR MARY SMITH

The main source for this story is Rev. H. Mattison, *The Abduction of Mary Ann Smith by the Roman Catholics, and her Imprisonment in a Nunnery for Becoming a Protestant* (Jersey City: published by the author, 1868). This book represents the Protestant point of view, but provides the text of the opposing Catholic view, if only to refute it.

18. MRS. STANTON STEPS OUT IN TENAFLY

A worthwhile book, published as a companion to the PBS documentary, is Geoffrey C. Ward (with contributors Martha Saxton and Ann Gordon), *Ourselves Alone: The Story of Elizabeth Cady Stanton and Susan B. Anthony* (New York: Alfred A. Knopf, 2001). Stanton's own words can be read in her book *Eighty Years and More: Reminiscences, 1815–1897*, with contributions by Ellen Carol DuBois and Ann Gordon (Lebanon, NH: University Presses of New England, 1993).

19. IT'S ABOUT TIME

The best book on the subject is Michael O'Malley, *Keeping Watch: A History of American Time* (New York: Viking, 1990).

20. LEPROSY IN THE LAUNDRY

This chapter is based on articles in New Jersey newspapers from 1888 to 1900. For a study of journalism in this era, see Ted Curtis Smythe, *The Gilded Age Press, 1865–1900* (Westport, CT: Praeger, 2003).

21. STEPHEN CRANE GETS INTO TROUBLE

The Asbury Park episode is covered in two works: R. W. Stallman, *Stephen Crane: A Biography* (New York: George Braziller, 1968); and John Berryman, *Stephen Crane: American Man of Letters* (n.p.: Sloane Associates, 1950). The Web site of the Stephen Crane Society is www.wsu.edu/~campbelld/crane/index.html.

22. THE GHOSTLY SPHYNX OF METEDECONK

The text of Crane's ghost stories and a keen analysis of those stories can be found in Daniel G. Hoffman, "Stephen Crane's New Jersey Ghosts: Two Newly Recovered Sketches," *Proceedings of the New Jersey Historical Society* 71 (October 1953): 239–253. This is the article that identifies Crane as the author of the newspaper stories. For a survey of classic New Jersey ghost stories, see Oral S. Coad, "Jersey Gothic," *Proceedings of the New Jersey Historical Society* 84 (1966): 89–112.

23. ANNIE OAKLEY LIVED IN NUTLEY, NEW JERSEY

A respected biography that examines the larger influence of Oakley is Glenda Riley, *The Life and Legacy of Annie Oakley* (Norman: University of Oklahoma Press, 1994). Another look at Oakley's place in history is Larry McMurtry, *The Colonel and Little Missie: Buffalo Bill, Annie Oakley and the Beginnings of Superstardom in America* (New York: Simon & Schuster, 2005). An article that sees Oakley as a breaker of stereotypes about women is Damaine Vonada, "Annie Oakley Was More Than 'A Crack Shot in Petticoats,'" *Smithsonian* (September 1990): 131–143

24. SCANDAL AT THE GIRLS' REFORM SCHOOL

The scandalous story of Matron Eyler is narrated in William Sackett, *Modern Battles of Trenton*, vol. 2, *From Werts to Wilson* (New York: Neale, 1914). A study of the kind of sensationalist reporting that characterized newspapers in that era is David Ralph Spencer, *The Yellow Journalism: The Press and America's Emergence as a World Power* (Evanston, IL: Northwestern University Press, 2007).

25. ALICE GOES FOR A DRIVE

Alice Ramsey wrote a book about her cross-country trip. The book was self-published and is difficult to find: *Veil, Duster, and Tire Iron* (Convina, CA, 1961). A book about the pioneering women motorists is Virginia Scharff, *Taking the Wheel: Women and the Coming of the Motor Age* (New York: Free Press, 1991).

26. BILLY SUNDAY CAME TO TRENTON ON MONDAY

A biography of the evangelist is Roger Bruns, *Billy Sunday and Big-Time American Evangelism* (New York: W. W. Norton, 1992). Another is Lyle W. Dorsett, *Billy Sunday and the Redemption of America* (Grand Rapids, MI: W. B. Erdmans, 1991).

27. EZRA POUND INSULTS NEWARK

The saga is recounted in J. J. Wilhelm, "Ezra Pound's Tribute to Newark," *New Jersey History* 104 (Fall/Winter 1986): 43–47. A book that explores Pound's fascist leanings is Tim Redman, *Ezra Pound and Italian Fascism* (Cambridge: Cambridge University Press, 1991).

28. CHER AMI

There are two books that tell you everything you want to know about pigeons, including the wartime service of Cher Ami: Wendell Mitchell Levi, *The Pigeon* (Sumter, SC: Levi, 1963) and Andrew Blechman, *Pigeons: The Fascinating Saga of the World's Most Revered and Reviled Bird* (New York: Grove Press, 2006).

29. THE POET, THE ATHLETE, AND THE WAR TO END ALL WARS

The following are useful biographies of the two principals in the story: Emil R. Salvini, *Hobey Baker: American Legend* (St. Paul, MN, Hobey Baker Memorial Foundation, 2005) and John E. Covell, *Joyce Kilmer: A Literary Biography* (Brunswick, GA: Write-Fit Communications, 2000).

30. THE APPLEJACK CAMPAIGN

The story of the election is well told in Warren E. Stickle III, "The Applejack Campaign of 1919: 'As Wet as the Atlantic Ocean,'" *New Jersey History* 90 (1972): 83–96.

31. SWAN SONG FOR SHOELESS JOE

A gripping account of the baseball scandal that destroyed Shoeless Joe's career is Eliot Asinof, *Eight Men Out: The Black Sox and the 1919 World Series* (New York: Holt, Reinhart & Winston, 1977). A book that focuses sympathetically on Jackson is Harvey Frommer, *Shoeless Joe and Ragtime Baseball* (Dallas: Taylor, 1992). A Web site that campaigns to have Jackson elected to the baseball Hall of Fame is the Shoeless Joe Jackson Virtual Hall of Fame, www.blackbetsy.com.

32. THE TRAGIC FALL OF THE MEXICAN LINDBERGH

This episode cries out for a larger study, but in the absence of such a study, anybody interested in learning more will have to read through contemporary newspaper accounts. Information about the Carranza memorial can be found in Meredith Bzdak, *Public Sculpture in New Jersey: Monuments to Collective Identity* (New Brunswick: Rutgers University Press, 1999).

33. ON THE BOARDWALK WITH AL CAPONE

A biography of Capone that delves into the Atlantic City convention is Luciano J. Iorizzo, *Al Capone: A Biography* (Westport, CT: Greenwood, 2003).

34. THE *MORRO CASTLE* MYSTERY

A well-written book on the subject is Thomas Michael Gallagher, *Fire at Sea: The Mysterious Tragedy of the Morro Castle* (Guilford, CT: Globe Pequot, 2003). Originally published in 1959, this was the first book to attribute the disaster to Rogers. A recent book that also accepts Rogers's guilt is Brian Hicks, *When the Dancing Stopped: The Real Story of the Morro Castle Disaster and Its Deadly Wake* (New York: Free Press, 2006).

35. THE RISE AND FALL OF A GREAT DETECTIVE

The story of the forced confession is contained in a book by the aggrieved party himself, Paul H. Wendel, *The Lindbergh-Hauptmann Aftermath* (Brooklyn: Loft, 1940). For a study of this case, see John Reisinger, *Master Detective: The Life and Crimes of Ellis Parker—America's Real-Life Sherlock Holmes* (New York: Citadel Press, 2006). The most authoritative work on the kidnapping is Jim Fisher, *The Lindbergh Case* (New Brunswick: Rutgers University Press, 1987).

36. MOMMY WAS A COMMIE

There is no book-length study of the *Eaton v. Eaton* case. A collection of primary sources, including legal documents and newspaper clippings, is contained in the American Civil Liberties Union papers at the Seeley G. Mudd Manuscript Library, Princeton University.

37. THE MARTIAN INVASION

Two good books on the subject are Handley Cantril et al., *The Invasion from Mars: A Study in the Psychology of Panic* (Princeton: Princeton University Press, 1940) and Howard Koch, *The Panic Broadcast: Portrait of an Event* (Boston: Little, Brown, 1970). The famous broadcast can be heard on the Web site www.mercurytheatre.info.

38. WHEN NEW JERSEY WAS A NAZI TARGET

A gripping book about the U-boat campaign is Michael Gannon, *Operation Drumbeat: The Dramatic True Story of Germany's First U-Boat Attack along the American Coast in World War II* (New York: Harper & Row, 1990). For a look at how the U-boat campaign fit in with the broader war effort, see the magisterial Samuel Eliot Morison, *History of United States Naval Operations in World War II*, 15 vols. (Urbana: University of Illinois Press, 2001–2002). In particular, volume 1 covers the Battle of the Atlantic. Readers interested in the connection between U-boats and New Jersey will enjoy Robert Kurson, *Shadow Divers: The True Adventure of Two Americans Who Risked Everything to Solve One of the Last Mysteries of World War II* (New York: Random House, 2004), which describes the discovery of the hulk of a German submarine that was destroyed in 1945, sixty miles off the Jersey coast.

39. TELEPORTING PENGUIN LANDS IN NEW JERSEY

For an entertaining early critique of Forteanism, see Martin Gardner, *Fads and Fallacies in the Name of Science* (New York: Courier Dover, 1957). The Web site of the International Fortean Society shows that the movement inspired by Fort is still very much alive: www.forteans.com.

40. THE SERPENT IN THE GARDEN STATE: A BRIEF HISTORY OF CORRUPTION

Anybody studying corruption in the nineteenth and early twentieth century in New Jersey needs to consult William Edgar Sackett, *Modern Battles of Trenton*, 2 vols. (Trenton: J. L. Murphy, 1895–1914). A lively tabloid-style approach is Jon Blackwell, *Notorious New Jersey: 100 True Tales of Murders and Mobsters, Scandals and Scoundrels* (New Brunswick: Rivergate Books, 2008).

INDEX

Italicized page numbers indicate illustrations.

population, 2–4, 189–190
Pound, Ezra, 127–130
Presbyterians, 6, 39, 41
Princeton, 53, 67, 137–138, 163, 184, 195
Progressive era, 175, 184–185
Prohibition, 102, 127, 139–142, 150, 184, 189
Proprietors, 6–7, 9
Pulaski Skyway, 164

Quakers, x, 6, 21, 83

Rahway, 172
Ramsey, Alice Huyler, 120–124, *121*
Reid, Whitlaw, 107–108
Reno, Marcus, 82–88
Republican Party, 60–62, 77, 80, 96, 107–108, 139, 140–142, 181–186, 188
Robeson, Paul, x
Rockingham, 46–49
Rockland, Michael, xi, 12
Rocky Hill, 46
Rodeheaver, Homer, 125
Roebling, John and Washington, ix
Rogers, George, 154–156
Roosevelt, Franklin, 130, 142, 162
Roosevelt, Theodore, 184
Ross, Betsy, 22–23, 25
Rutgers University, 4–5, 12, 15, 49, 127, 135, 191, 194–195

Sackett, William, 118, 178, 182–183
Saint Mary's Hall school, 79
Saks, Raven, 189
Salem County, 62–65, 179
Sawyer, Harriet, 70, 72–74
Sawyer, Henry, 70–74, 77, *71*
Schlossman, Martin, 158
Sea Girt, 153
Sea Isle City, 168
Sewell, William, 183
Sherman, William Tecumseh, 70
Sickler, Joseph, 65
Sinatra, Frank, x, 5, 14, 193
Sitting Bull, 114

slavery, 50–53, 67, 94–95
Sloanmaker, H. L., 88
Smith, Andrew F., 63
Smith, James, 90–92
Smith, Mary Ann, 90–93
Society for the Encouragement of Useful Manufactures, 176–177
Somers, Richard, 66
Somerville, 101
Sopranos, The (TV series), ix, x, 12
South Amboy, 185
Spanish-American War, 108, 118
Springsteen, Bruce, 12, 14, 193
Stanton, Edwin M., 80–81
Stanton, Elizabeth Cady, 93–97, *94*
Steffens, Lincoln, 175, 184, 188
Stern, Herbert, 186
Stevens, John, 4–5
Stevenson, Robert Louis, 89
Stickle, Warren, 142
Stockton, Robert, 66–69
Sunday, Billy, 124–127
Sussex County, 15, 102–103

Tenafly, 93–97
Tiffany, J. Raymond, 162
tomatoes, 62–66
Trenton, 15, 23, 53, 73, 99, 105, 116–120, 124–127, 128, 139, 140, 142, 155, 157, 165, 172, 182, 184
Tyler, John, 67–69
Tyler, Robert, 72–73

U-boats, 168–171
Union City, 187
Union County, 39, 187
Union Township, 38
United States Life Saving Service, 73–74
Upshur, Abel, 69
USS *Princeton*, 66–69
Utley, Robert, 86

Van Wart, Isaac, 45
Verrazzano, Giovanni da, 1

ABOUT THE AUTHOR

Marc Mappen was the coeditor of the *Encyclopedia of New Jersey* and has written other books about United States and New Jersey history. He has written articles for the *New York Times*, the *Los Angeles Times*, *Rutgers Magazine*, and other publications. He has appeared on the History Channel and been interviewed on National Public Radio. Mappen has a Ph.D. in American history and was an associate dean at Rutgers University prior to his retirement. He lives in (where else?) New Jersey.